War, Love, and Redemption
A Memoir

by
Katrina Čakste Wilson

Cover Artist – Becky Reiser
Storybridge Media
RĀBAR PRODUCTIONS

"One generation commands Your works to another;
they tell of your mighty acts." Psalms 145:4

ISBN: 979-8-9879862-0-2

The Parish Press
Keller, TX
Printed in the United States of America

PATRONS

The Rev. Cn. and Mrs. Rob P. Smith
The Rt. Rev. Ryan S. Reed
The Rev. and Mrs. H. David Wilson
Mr. and Mrs. Langley Granbery
Mr. and Mrs. Charles C. Smith
Mr. and Mrs. Charles L. Kown
Mr. and Mrs. Bob McElwee
Mr. Walter Virden, III

DEDICATION

In loving memory of
Professor Konstantins Jakobs Čakste
and
Anastasija Stipnieks Čakste

My parents on whose shoulders I stand.

ACKNOWLEDGEMENTS

My heart is full of gratitude and appreciation for my husband, the Rev. Harold David Wilson. Without his help and encouragement this book may not yet be finished. Some months before the world was locked down by the Covid virus, when in my time of morning prayer and meditation, I heard the Holy Spirit say, "Write." I didn't have a computer. I was a public speaker, not a writer. When I told my husband that the Lord wanted me to write, he said, "Well let's go get you a computer; you won't be able to do a book on your iPad." He taught me how to use that darn thing and he spent countless hours reading and rereading chapter after chapter. Thank you my love, my gift; you have been the wind in my sails.

Our daughter, Anastasia Brown, has been an invaluable aide and source of information since she has published innumerable articles as well as a book. Anastasia, I appreciate all the times you worked with me as I began to write. Your coaching helped me to open up my heart to my readers so that I might bring them along on my journey. I greatly appreciated your sensitive, joyful, loving spirit as you encouraged and affirmed my work. Thank you Dear for writing the Foreword. I love you to the furthest star and back.

I wish to acknowledge my sister, Anna Rollins. We have experienced so much of this journey together. I have been blessed by the love and friendship we have shared throughout the years. Thank you, dear sister.

Freddy Richardson, a free-lance writer and author, corrected the first draft of this book. Thank you for the sage advice and your words of affirmation. Praise from you was indeed a great encouragement.

I want to acknowledge and thank friends who read early portions of this work in progress: Becky Smith, who herself was working on a book, and Martha Elkin, a sage and very effective teacher of Ladies' Bible Studies, and Sheila Erwin, author of the book, *Raising Up Dreamers*, your prayers, advice, and affirmation kept me on task. I need to acknowledge many other friends, too numerous to name, individuals who have over the years recommended that I write this story, even offered to write it for me. You have been an encouragement and your faith that my story can be a blessing to those who read it has given me confidence to persevere. Thank you, dear friends.

Also, I want to thank the Franklin Christian Authors' group. Each time I was invited to read a portion of my manuscript you were affirming and encouraging. Praise from experienced and published authors was the fuel I needed to keep going.

I want to acknowledge the great help I found from the Library of Congress in Washington, D.C. Having heard so many amazing stories of historic interest from my mother, I needed to confirm the accuracy of my recollection of her tales before writing them into a book. The Library of Congress made that possible. For instance, mother's recollection of Hitler's speech was confirmed as I listened to a translation of one of his speeches that had been recorded on vinyl. The library is a treasure of easily accessible information of history. I am indebted to this rich resource.

Finally, I am never surprised by God's inspired activity but always humbly grateful. One morning in early March, Dave hung up on an unfamiliar mobile phone number, but when it rang again right away, he answered and was surprised to hear the cheerful voice of Bishop Keith Ackerman's greeting. How the Bishop tracked down Dave's cell phone number, I do not know. We don't have a house phone anymore and it had been many years since we had been in touch. He remembered that I was born in Latvia and was excited to tell us about his work with Latvian Bishops and Clergy. When I told him that I had written my Memoir, he enthusiastically asked if he and Joann could read it. I warned him that it still had some errors in punctuation and spelling, but he told me not to worry about that. I emailed it to them not knowing that his talented wife was a publisher with The Parish Press. After they read my work, they offered to publish it. I want to express my deepest gratitude to Bishop and Joann for the work of correcting, formatting, registering, and publishing the work of our Lord's amazing grace in my life. I am awestruck by His provision. Thank you from the bottom of my heart dear friends.

FOREWORD

My Mother's Memoir is about one family's attempt to survive while governments waged war and people were judged by the color of their eyes but most importantly, the powerful story about true love and steadfast faith.

I learned about the Čakste history as a young child and in turn shared those profound stories with my son, Wilson Konstantine. We craved to know our ancestors, those we never knew. Sometimes I hesitated telling him the frightening stories about the terrors our ancestors experienced. But then I stopped to think — my mother and her sister actually experienced the very real nightmare that we are witnessing on TV with the Ukrainian refugee crisis at the same young age. As a mother myself, I reflect with amazement at the strength of our matriarch, Anastasija Čakste, whom, as a woman in her 30's and 40's, became a widow, single mother, refugee and then a successful meteorologist and librarian in America. Prior to that she led a dangerous escape plan from the Nazi's and most importantly, saved her children from the nightmares found in all concentration camps throughout Europe. What brings me to tears every time, when I let my mind wander in this direction, is the thought of Anastajia having to leave her husband in a concentration camp, her parents and country behind completely alone; all to protect her little babies.

The people in my mother's memoir are not fictional — they are our family and friends. The experiences she shares are real, inspiring and heartbreaking; it is a story about her life from a small, beautiful country along the Baltic Sea. It goes deep into history, from WWII, when Hitler and Stalin traded countries as if they were playing chess, into the aftermath of those dictators' destruction. It was a time when men and women of Eastern Europe had no experience with a free world. Nevertheless, her grandfather, Jānis Čakste, the first President of Latvia, knew he must fight for a free world. Even time spent in a Russian prison did not divert him from that goal. Although the size of this country was small, the battle he fought and won against an overpowering tyrant was felt around the world. Seventy years after his death Jānis was inducted into the Hall of Freedom as one of the most influential men in the history of the world to bring an end to oppression, along with Abraham

Lincoln, Gandhi, and Winston Churchill. He left a legacy of democracy—freedom for all.

His son, Konstantine, fought the next battle. This war devastated our family which took fifty years to overcome. While my mother's father loved his family dearly, he refused to consent to a future without freedom for his children. So, he created the underground government, Latvia's Central Council. Even after exhausting all of his personal resources and being included on the ominous "black list," he didn't back down, he pushed harder. In consequence, Hitler captured him which is when my mother and her family were forced to sail first to Sweden and then to America and Ellis Island as refugees. But what I am most affected and inspired by is the strength of our family. They stand as proof that one person's dream, passion, and determination can change history.

I am beyond proud that my mother wrote her memoir. It isn't a small task. Yet I am not surprised, as God called her to write her story and she always follows His Word. It's also important for her to share her truth so history cannot be erased nor repeated. It is from this nightmare and her incredible life I learned about personal heroes and heroines.

Our family history has influenced my thoughts and shaped my life so much I am thrilled you get to read about it. Hearing these stories throughout my life gave me the understanding that true love does exist, heroes walk among us and there is, for certain, a Higher Power.

I love you Mom, well done; I know Ama, Papa, and Jānis are proud.

Xoxo
Anastasia Wilson Brown

War, Love, and Redemption

A Memoir

by

Katrina Čakste Wilson

TABLE OF CONTENTS **Page**

Chapter One: *THE PHONE CALL - 1991 Florida USA…………1*

Chapter Two: *1938 - THE YEAR OF MY BIRTH – JURMALA….6*

Chapter Three: *THE SECOND WORLD WAR - 1944 RIGA…….13*

Chapter Four: *THE SOVIET OCCUPATION OF LATVIA………23*

Chapter Five: *COULD I BE A KILLER AT THE AGE OF FIVE?28*

Chapter Six: *HEAVEN IS NEAR……………………………………39*

Chapter Seven: *EXILED IN SWEDEN – 1944…………………47*

Chapter Eight: *IN THE SHADOW OF DEATH – 1945…………50*

Chapter Nine: *SAILING ACROSS THE ATLANTIC……………72*

Chapter Ten: *REFUGEES ON ELLIS ISLAND…………………81*

Chapter Eleven: *AMERICA…………………………………………85*

Chapter Twelve: *DISCOVERING A NEW HOME………………89*

Chapter Thirteen: *THE LOSS OF INNOCENCE………………94*

Chapter Fourteen: *GROWING UP……………………………100*

Chapter Fifteen: *SURPRISED BY LOVE………………………108*

Chapter Sixteen: *A NAVY WIFE – 1962………………………123*

Chapter Seventeen: *VIETNAM - MY HUSBAND CALLED TO SERVE IN WAR………………………………………………127*

Chapter Eighteen: *DAVE UNDER FIRE………………………134*

Chapter Nineteen: *"I AM HE WHOM THOU SEEKEST"……139*

Chapter Twenty: *A NEW CAREER & GROWING IN FAITH…145*

Chapter Twenty-One: *RETURN TO LATVIA – 1989…………161*

Chapter Twenty-Two: *REDEMPTION, RESTORATION AND RENEWAL……………………………………………………170*

ENDORSEMENTS…………………………………………………185

Chapter One: *THE PHONE CALL - 1991 Florida USA*

On an early fall evening in Florida the sun had painted the sky with bright colors of crimson, coral, and violet. It reflected every shade of pink on the surface of the water of our pool. I stood mesmerized, admiring this beautiful scene with my pruning shears in my hand, when the insistent ringing of the phone interrupted my rumination. I dashed into our little kitchen to answer the cream-colored phone that hung on the cream-colored wall beneath our cream-colored kitchen cabinet. Picking up the receiver I wanted to say, "Hello and praise God on this glorious evening" but I had learned from my mistakes in the past to answer the phone properly. The first year of my transition from a Navy pilot's wife to a minister's wife, I had grabbed the phone in a jolly mood and said, "Hello on this glorious day." That was followed by a few moments of silence and then a shaking voice inquired for Father Dave, my husband. Her son had been killed driving home from college. It was not a glorious day for her, and I learned my lesson. So instead, I said, "Hello, the Wilson residence."

On this glorious day the surprise was on me. The unfamiliar voice on the other end of the line asked, "Hello, are you Mrs. Wilson?" "Yes, may I ask who is calling?" I replied, feeling puzzled. "I am Leons Panics. You don't know me, but I am calling because I am trying to find the whereabouts of Katrina Wilson, the daughter or Konstantins Čakste," he replied.

At the mention of my late father's name, I was dumbstruck. I felt my throat tighten, and I pulled out the kitchen stool to sit down. My father was my hero, and I had never stopped missing him. My heart began to beat more rapidly just hearing his name from a stranger. I said, "Yes, Konstantins Čakste was my father. Why do you ask?" "I am so happy to have reached you, Mrs. Wilson," Mr. Pancis continued. "I am alive because your father, Professor Čakste, saved my life." I could not speak - I was momentarily in shock. After a few moments of silence, he went on, "Let me explain. At the age of twenty, I was a student at the University of Latvia's School of Law in Riga, when in 1941 the Nazis arrested me along with all the other Latvian Jewish students." I knew about the terrible Jewish ghetto prison established during the Nazi occupation of Riga. "In late September of 1944, I was shipped to Stutthof Concentration Camp in Germany." *He lived thorough Stutthof?* I thought in disbelief. At the time I had not met anyone who had lived through Stutthof and knew my father. Mr. Pancis continued, "In the camp I learned that a prominent Latvian professor was incarcerated there, who was the son of the first president of Latvia. In the belief and hope that it was my favorite professor, your father, and that he would remember me, I sought him out as he walked from barrack to barrack checking on the Latvian prisoners."

I finally regained my voice and breathlessly asked, "You knew my father, you saw him in Stutthof?" Mr. Pancis then told me the whole story. "*Yes, I did know your father. When I approached him in the camp, I was relieved that he remembered me and invited me to walk along with him. As we walked throughout the camp, one of the guards yelled at him, "What are you doing with that Jew?" Your father calmly replied, "Mr. Panics was one of my students," putting his hand on my shoulder, indicating to me I should keep walking. As we walked, he asked me what jobs I was assigned. I told him that, although I raised my hand at roll call, I was never given a job. Your father then told me that meant I had been assigned to the ovens (meaning being gassed to death and then burned). "We have to attempt to get you out of here, you have nothing to lose," he said. He told me that he would scout all possible escape routes and contact me. As we shook hands, he smuggled a piece of bread in my hand. Maybe because he was considered a celebrity prisoner, he had a way to get extra food?"*

"A couple of days later, when a group of Nazis from Potentate Ammunition Factory arrived to procure some fresh workers at early morning roll call, I raised my hand again and was not picked. Under the cover of darkness, I made my way to Professor Čakste. He smuggled me into his barracks, gave me bread tied up in a handkerchief, and told me his plan. He had managed to pry open the little window in his barracks just enough for a malnourished, skinny young man like me to squeeze through. He believed I could blend in with the prisoners who had already been counted and were standing with their backs to the barracks, ready to be shipped to work in the ammunition factory. Then he warned me that I would need to get out of that column before it arrived at the train station, where another roll call would be taken. He said I should keep

heading west towards the setting sun. He led me to the little window in the back of his barracks and helped me squeeze through an opening no wider than my head. I slid down and lost myself in the column of prisoners and marched out as if I belonged. Outside the gate, there were a lot of soldiers and dogs guarding us as we walked toward the train station. Fortunately for me, there was a major disturbance that distracted the guards and the dogs away from me. I don't know if someone had fallen or tried to escape. I took the opportunity and dove into the underbrush, lying silent and still, waiting until the column of skeletal men passed by. If I had been caught your father and I both would have been killed. I owe my life to Professor Čakste, and I wanted to find some way to honor him. I read an article in the newspaper about your work to host the Riga Dome Boys Choir and your visit to Latvia with your mother and sister. It did not mention whether your father was alive. Did he survive the camp?"

By this time, I was stretching the line of the wall phone trying to reach a paper towel to dry my eyes and nose, after clearing my throat, I said, "No, no. He didn't survive." Mr. Panics' voice sounded gentler as if he were far away, perhaps his mind had taken him back to that narrow windowsill in the back of my Papa's barracks. Then he told me how very sorry he was to hear that news, and he asked me if he could have my mother's address so he could write to her. "Yes, of course, but tell me, how did you survive after that?" I asked. He continued. *A kind German family discovered me asleep in their barn and helped me at great risk, even though they were obviously afraid to be discovered helping me. I spoke fluent German, so we could communicate. They ran to the house and brought me clothes that had belonged to their son, who had died in the "senseless war" as they described it. They kept saying, "Quickly, quickly (schnell, schnell)," as I hurried to get out of my prison pajamas and put on civilian clothes. Then they threw my prison pajamas into a roaring fire in a barrel, which they kept poking, adding garden waste to the barrel to ensure that no scrap of my prison pajamas would remain to be discovered. The next night I kept moving west like your father told me to do."*

"By the grace of God," I whispered, then I gave him Mama's address and said goodbye. My mind was whirling like a tornado in my head. I felt like I had heard a voice from beyond the grave. A cloud had descended over the beautiful evening outside the window. I pondered: *Was it his love of Latvia's youth, of Latvia's future? Is that why my father gave that young man his bread and later died of starvation, disease, and brutality?* There was no way for anyone to get extra food in Stutthof Concentration Camp.

When the USSR troops approached East Germany (now Poland) where the camp was located, the prisoners were driven westward through knee deep snow in blizzard conditions. A chunk of bread was given to each prisoner, intended to last them a week. At night, just as in the camp, soup was cooked with whatever the SS soldiers could conscript - mostly water, a potato or two for the entire barrel, and horse meat. No one escaped suffering from diarrhea. Typhoid and meningitis were rampant among the prisoners. Anyone who could not keep pace marching westward was first bitten by the dogs and then shot by the SS. Starving, sick, and frozen, not many survived. With a heavy heart I sat immobile on that kitchen stool after I hung up the phone, picturing in my mind the horror and suffering my father had endured.

I was still sitting there, lost in my thoughts, when my husband, Dave, came home. Dashing in from the garage he gave me a passing air kiss and said, "Sorry I'm late, I was held up. I'll be ready in ten." *Oh no!* I thought to myself. We are supposed to go to a party, a surprise party, to which we had RSVP'd, but I couldn't move. I felt like I had just spoken with a voice from beyond the grave.

The little child inside this middle-aged body wanted to cry, "Why, Papa, didn't you keep your word? You told me you would be back. You helped that man survive, but you didn't?"
I hadn't felt those emotions since I was a little girl sitting through memorial services for my Dad. Now they were resurrected, casting a heavy blanket of grief over me, and I was supposed to go to a party and be merry?

All through the party and afterwards I ruminated about the phone call, my father, and how deeply he loved Latvia and her people. I resolved that I needed to help, in his stead, in the rebuilding of a free and democratic Latvia. Secondly, I wanted to go to Stutthof concentration camp. I wanted to find some remains, if possible, of Papa's earthly body to bring back to Latvia, in the hopes that even a bone or two of his could rest where his ancestors have rested since the sixteenth century in Latvia's rich black soil. With those thoughts rumbling around in my brain I slept restlessly. “I'm here, Papa!” I shouted out loud in my sleep. That awakened me from my nightmare. I turned over to see Dave sleeping soundly beside me and reached for him, for the comfort and peace that touching him imbued. The phone call had brought me back to Latvia in the Second World War.

Oh, my heavenly Father, I thought prayerfully. *Into this life of tears, you have brought so much joy, so much love. Thank you, thank you, Lord of Love.*

Chapter Two: *1938 - THE YEAR OF MY BIRTH - JURMALA*

For you created my inmost being; you knit me together in my mother's womb.
Psalm 139:13

Konstantin hummed a folk song as he walked out the door of our summer cottage which was located on the shore of the Baltic Sea. Anna, his two and a half years old daughter dashed out after him, her arms outstretched calling for him, "Papa, Papa?" He stopped, turned around and reached down to pick her up, "I'm going to take the train to Riga. I'll bring your new sister and Mama home tonight," he told her as he swung her around and planted a kiss on her forehead. Then he handed her to the nurse who had followed them out the door and continued on his way humming as he walked. The warm sea breeze rustling the needles of the ancient, tall pine trees that lined the shore of the Baltic Sea, seemed to be harmonizing with his familiar song.

Konstantin loved children and would have been glad to have a quiver full of them. Yet he and his, beloved Anastasija, had to wait four years after they were married in 1932 to welcome Anna. Therefore, when I rushed into the world early, two and half years after Anna's birth, he was delighted. Mamma and I remained in the hospital for ten days. Today at last, just a few days before his birthday, Konstantin was on his way to bring us home. As he walked, he passed his brother, Mintauts', house and spotted Aja, his teenage niece, in the garden. "Aja" he called, "would you please go to the florist and purchase every flower in the shop and decorate our house from top to bottom. I am on my way to bring Anastasija and our new daughter home," he said, handing her a wad of money. Aja was excited to take on the important responsibility of purchasing the flowers and decorating the house for the newest Čakste. She was very fond of Konstantin and Anastasija. Aja was a pianist and spent several hours practicing every day. She loved classical music. Recognizing her love of music Konstantin and Anastasija had often invited her to accompany them to performances of an opera or symphony.

Aja once told me that she loved to observe the look on Konstantin's face when he was looking at Anastasija. "I attended several concerts with them when they were newly married, that gave me the opportunity to study their relationship, their devotion to each other was visceral. I noticed that sometimes Konstantin walked behind Anastasija and I asked him why? He smiled as he responded 'I like to watch her walk, look how beautifully her dress sways from side to side'. Everyone in the family talked about how helplessly those two where in love," Aja recalled.

After giving Aja money to purchase flowers, Konstantin continued on his way to the train station. In Riga he was met by his friend and brother-in-law Paulis Zemgalis. Paulis had offered to meet him and drive all of them home to Jurmala from the hospital. Paulis' wife, Daila, was Konstantin's youngest sister and had been Anastasija's dear friend since childhood, she would be coming too. She wanted to help Anastasija and join the welcome home festivities.

Anastasija was very fond of Daila, "Daila and I were two young girls, still wearing pigtails, when I met Konstantin. He was attending Latvia's University of Law. I often visited Daila, who, with her family, lived in Riga's Castle," Mama told me. Jānis Čakste, their father, was the first democratically elected President of Latvia; the family living quarters were in the castle as well as the official presidential offices and receiving rooms.

"One afternoon when I was visiting Daila, two of her brothers, Konstantin and Ringolds, came into the room where Daila and I were now doing homework. They were dressed in their evening suits ready for a fraternity ball, I thought they looked so handsome, I was smitten. I felt a little shy and nervously laughed at their friendly banter. Oh my, after they left Daila and I talked about how much we looked forward to the day when we would be old enough to go to university and attend Balls." "Is that when you fell in love with Papa?" "I admired him. I was much too young to know about love — that came later," she said, her eyes sparkling, and I saw the faraway look that sometimes came across her face when I questioned her about her youth.

"Mama, I recall seeing a picture of you riding a horse and a dog standing beside you who looked tall enough to be a colt. Tell me about that picture?" I asked. "I loved to ride! I was a good rider, if I say so myself. In the wintertime at Auci, when the river was frozen over, I was the one who was asked to cantor my horse down the frozen river towing one or two skiers behind me, you know, the same way that a boat pulls skiers across the water." "That must have been so much fun. What about the dog in the picture? I don't remember seeing a dog like that." "His name was Cesar. Your Papa came to visit me soon after I accepted his proposal for marriage; he came in with a big grin on his face and took a little puppy out of his coat pocket and presented him to me. That little puppy grew up to be that big, handsome great Dane." "He was beautiful." "Your Papa had a witty sense of humor," Mamma told me in response to my questions. She nodded her head and a little smile formed on her lips as she said that. I smiled as well noticing that happy memories must have been resurrected in her mind.

"What happened to Cesar?" I asked. "In the early years of our marriage, before we had children, I traveled with your Papa when he attended meetings on international law and economics in other European Capitals. We left Cesar with my parents; they enjoyed him, and he was a good guard dog for Ama's store. In 1939 and '40 the uncertainty of life under the Soviet occupation caused crime to rise, and many stores experienced break-ins. Ama would leave Cesar in her store overnight, and she never had a problem. However, Cesar ate a lot. We would prepare, what you might call, a big pot of stew for him every week. Under the occupation food in the city became scarce so my parents had to take Cesar to relatives who had a farm." "Oh, that's so sad, I bet you missed him?" "Yes, I did but he was so big; when I returned home from a trip his enthusiasm would overwhelm him. He would stand on his back legs, put his front paws around my neck, I would have to brace myself against a wall so as not to fall down under his weight. The farm was a good place for him; he was a good guard dog for them. Russian soldiers took one look at him and never molested them. But just a few days after he was gone from Ama's store it was robbed." "That's too bad, I wish I had memories of Caesar, I've always loved dogs," I said, feeling nostalgic.

My parents had purchased the land in Jurmala soon after their marriage in 1932. Jurmala is a little slice of paradise on the western shore of the Baltic Sea. It is only a thirty-minute train ride from Riga but it feels like a different world. Once you leave the hustle and bustle of the 800-year-old capital city of Latvia and arrive in the beach community the fragrance of the sea air mingled with the scent of pine trees greets you, welcomes you. The air is so fresh and fragrant. They had purchased a large lot and built a small cottage in one corner of the lot to enjoy during the warm weather and perhaps retire there someday, far in the future. Konstantin had asked a friend of his, who was an architect, to design the house. They thought perhaps sometime in the future, if they had many children, they may need a larger home, which the lot would accommodate. Behind the house were sand dunes, pine trees, and the shore of the Baltic Sea. All spring and summer our family lived in this idyllic setting, conveniently located, an easy commute from Riga.

Latvia was reborn and became a Constitutional Democracy at the end of the First World War. The 1920's were years of restoration and formation of a Democracy for Latvia. As the economy was based on agriculture, fishing, and boat building at the time, it did not suffer the ripple effects of the Great Depression in the US, after the collapse of the Stock Market in America. The early 1930s, when my parents married, were years of growth and increasing prosperity in Latvia. My parents envisioned someday retiring to the beautiful piece of land they had purchased.

Anastasija had studied and trained in ballet with some renowned ballerinas throughout her childhood and continued the lessons once she entered University where she studied economics and library science. The ballet was still her greatest passion however; therefore, she was absolutely thrilled when it was announced that she was cast to perform with the national ballet company in the Opera "Aida." Anastasija didn't know it, but "Aida" was Konstantin's favorite Opera. A picture of Anastasija was prominently displayed in store windows announcing the upcoming production. As he rarely missed an opera, I wonder did Papa's heart quicken when he saw his young friend, all grown up, performing on stage? I wish I could have asked him when he first became attracted to Mamma. Actually, there are many, many questions I have wanted to ask him throughout the ensuing years.

I am happy to have been told stories about my parents' love affair and the joyful celebration that surrounded my birth into the world. I was a longed-for child, warmly welcomed into the bosom of a large extended family. Nevertheless, in 1938 a dark cloud of concern was heavy at the back of their minds

Papa had many international connections at the University of Berlin, Brussels, and the Sorbonne in Paris. Having studied abroad he maintained relationships with the European intellectuals involved with creating laws for international commerce and establishing the League of Nations. His finger was on the pulse. While the world was still in denial about Hitler's intentions in 1938, the level of concern within Papa's inner circle was growing. In Germany, Hitler had abolished the War Ministry and instead created the High Command of the Armed Forces, giving him direct control of the German military. Thereby he was able to dismiss all military officers who expressed concern about his aggressive policies. Hitler had already marched into Austria and proclaimed a political and geographical union of Germany and Austria. Next, he threatened Czechoslovakia. What had concerned Papa was that Britain, France, and Italy agreed to let Germany partition that sovereign country.

In the fall of 1938, when the warm summer breezes were displaced by the chill of autumn, our family vacated our summer cottage and returned to our apartment in Riga, the capital City of Latvia. Mamma's father, Apap, often came for visits and to talk politics with Papa. Apap was a businessman and banker. One day in November he came over and was very agitated. "Hitler is a mad man! His followers, the Nazis, rioted all day and night in Berlin yesterday. They destroyed synagogues, they threw bricks through so many windows of Jewish owned shops and homes that glass covered all the sidewalks. Those Nazis hooligans had free reign to brutalize their Jewish neighbors. The police must have been instructed not to interfere," he said.

"Yes, I heard about that as well, but I don't think Hitler is a mad man. He is a shrewd atheist, ambitious and deceptive. I think he, like Stalin, wants to dominate the world". The three of them, Mama, Papa, and Apap looked downcast, lost in their thoughts for several moments. Then Apap broke the silence, "A neighbor of mine, with many business connections in Germany, is convinced war is coming to Latvia. He is leaving and moving to Palestine. I think we need to prepare, in whatever way we can, for war before it's on our doorstep." he told my parents.

The night that the Nazis in Germany commenced their brutal attack of their Jewish citizens, when broken glass covered the sidewalks, shimmering like crystals in the light of street-lamps, became known as Kristallnacht. With all this bad news coming out of Germany under Hitler's authoritarian domination, can you imagine my father's surprise and shock, when at the end of 1938, Time magazine in America had Hitler's picture on their cover declaring him to be "Man of the Year."

Anastasija Stipnieks Čakste
1932

Konstantin Čakste
Law School

Anastasija Stipnieks performed with the National Ballet Company in the Opera "Aida."

The Čakste Family - 1943

Chapter Three: *THE SECOND WORLD WAR - 1944 RIGA LATVIA*

"This is a war of the Unknown Warriors; but let all strive without failing in faith or in duty and the dark curse of Hitler will be lifted from our age." Winston Churchill

I was a very inquisitive child, and by the age of five I had overheard enough to be concerned for Papa's safety. Papa, Konstantin Čakste, was a professor of law and economics at the University of Latvia School of Law, in Riga. He was soft spoken, very tall, strong, and gentle, with a witty sense of humor and a *can-do* optimistic approach to life. Every time he came home joy, peace, and security flooded our home. Mother, Anastasija, was eight years his junior. She was beautiful, slender, and energetic. She was the disciplinarian and the one who made certain Anna, my sister who was two and a half years older, and I had teachers who came to our home. She made sure that we studied, ate healthy food, and that Papa had one or two delicious desserts every day. Mama had added the Study of Law to her impressive academic achievements, after she became engaged to Papa. Sometimes I could see concern written across her face when she and Papa were in a serious private conversation.

Riga, the capital city of Latvia was founded in the 12th century, and in 1940 through 1941 was occupied by Stalin's Russian forces. In 1941, the Nazi Army easily defeated the Russian Forces and began an occupation that lasted until the end of WWII (at which time Russia tried to annex the country.) Thick black curtains had been added to all the windows of our home so that bombers, flying through the night sky, would not see the lights of the city. After sunset no lampposts were lit, and buses and official vehicles moved about in the dark. Soon all private vehicles were confiscated; and if not, there was no petrol available for private use. The invading army needed it all.

After the Nazis occupied Latvia in 1941, all the newspapers were ordered to print headlines, in large, bold print, saying that the Nazis had liberated Latvia from the horror of the Soviet occupation of 1940, and what a year of horror it had been! The Nazis displayed the bodies of people tortured to death by the Soviet KGB. They laid them out in row after row on a football field: bodies of men, women, and boys. Some had nails protruding from their heads, some with swollen faces, missing teeth or tongues, some with fingers, toes, or genitals cut off. Each one had been brutally tortured to death and had been someone who was loved and missed and mourned. Families who had been worried about the disappearance of a relative, a relative who had not arrived home one day during the year of Stalin's occupation, were now invited to walk up and down the rows of those tortured corpses seeking to find out if one of their own had met that awful fate.

Aunt Marta, whose brother was the chief editor of the most prominent newspaper in Riga, was very concerned about her brother. He had disappeared during the Soviet occupation. She asked her sister-in-law, Aunt Irma, who was a medical doctor, if she would go to the football stadium and search for her brother's remains. Aunt Marta didn't know what had happened to her brother, but if his remains could be found she wanted him to have a proper burial. Aunt Irma walked up and down row after row of badly tortured corpses with her mouth and nose covered with a perfumed handkerchief. She said that it was the sheer force of willpower that kept her legs moving until she exited the stadium. Outside the stadium she collapsed in tears and vomited. Irma was a doctor who had performed autopsies as part of her medical training, nevertheless the unimaginable brutality against humanity she had seen was physically and emotionally traumatizing. Sadly, she didn't find Aunt Marta's brother. We never learned what happened to him after the KGB wanted to talk to him. Hitler's Nazi Army had defeated the Soviets so swiftly in July of 1941 that the Soviets had not been able to bury all of the evidence of their heinous brutality.

As soon as the Nazis set up their occupation Government, the radio blared "Heil Hitler! Citizens of Latvia, Hitler has liberated you; resume your normal lives." Some Latvian people, who did not have international connections, therefore, didn't know about Nazi brutality. They felt a sense of relief. The fear and suffering they had lived with during the Soviet occupation was over, they thought.

Mother, my sister, Anna, and I moved back to our own summer cottage and soon Papa came home from wherever he had been working underground during the Soviet occupation and brought us delicious cherries. I was only three years old at that time, nevertheless, I recall that joyful reunion. It was not the usual homecoming of our Papa; I think that's why I recall it. The picture I have in my mind's eye is of Mama smiling with tears running down her cheeks embracing Papa who was holding her with one arm while holding up the flat of cherries in the other. Anna and I ran to them and hugged them both, our arms wrapped around their legs. At my tender age I thought there was something special about those cherries. I was too young to understand the danger we were living in, and the danger we had survived. Papa was so relieved at seeing us, overjoyed that we were not deported. Mama was relieved that Papa had not been found by the KGB and that he had not been swept up in the battle that briefly raged between the Nazis and the retreating Russian Army. They had been living by the faith that they would survive and be reunited. All I understood at age three was the great joy of our reunited family. Papa was home with pretty, delicious cherries! Shops were opened and sweet pastries were once again available. For the rest of the summer, Papa resumed his routine of taking the train to Riga in the morning and coming home each night.

Because of our geographic location, the Latvian people had survived many occupations. To the east of Latvia is Russia, to the north is Estonia and Finland, to the south is Lithuania, Poland, and Germany, and to the west is the Baltic Sea. Across the Baltic Sea is Sweden. By nature, the Latvians are independent, industrious, and faithful to their ancient heritage, which dates back to before the Bronze Age. The root of the Latvian language is Sanskrit — it's one of the oldest living languages in Europe. The Latvian people cherish their culture, and believe that foreign rulers, occupying their land from time to time, coveting their rich agricultural soil and deep-water port to the Baltic Sea, will eventually be gone and their culture and language will live on.

In 1940, when Latvia suffered under the Soviet occupation, Papa had started an underground newspaper as well as the work of uniting all the resistance movements in Latvia into one. It eventually was called LCP (*Latvijas Centrālā Padome*, translated "Latvian Central Council"). He worked to forge a united front with resistance movements in the other Baltic countries: Estonia and Lithuania. All of this had to be done person to person, because mail could be intercepted, opened, and read. The telephone was also unreliable, as the Soviet KGB and the Nazi SS had spies listening to private conversations. University students, who Papa trusted, risked their lives to bring letters across the borders and later by boat to the Latvian Embassy in Sweden.

In the fall, when we returned to Riga and Papa resumed presenting his lectures at the University, Mama reorganized the nursery. A desk, a blackboard, and an upright piano were moved in. Anna was old enough to start first grade. My parents had decided that because of the occupation of Latvia it was not safe to send us to school. They decided we should both be homeschooled. Mama hired teachers to come to our home. We had a French Mademoiselle and a German Fraulein and our dear nanny "Bubulit." "Bubulit" was her endearing name for us, soon after getting to know her, it became the name we called her. When she arrived at our apartment she would bubble with enthusiasm,

"Good morning Bubulit," she might say, her eyes sparkling, "today we are going to have so much fun learning multiplication." She would turn recitation of letters and numbers into songs; she was a smiling ray of sunshine. I don't recall her given name because I always thought of her, with fondness, as Bubulit. After a happy year of homeschooling, Mademoiselle was the first one of our teachers to come and say goodbye. She did not possess her normal happy demeanor when talking to Mother in hushed tones. A year later Fraulein came to say that she had to return to Germany. We hugged and kissed her goodbye and then watched as tears trickled down her cheeks as she spoke to Mama.

I recalled the walks we took, accompanied by Papa. Often, I had to run beside him to keep up. When out for a walk, we usually met men along the way who wanted to speak with Papa. The purpose for these walks was to communicate with people in the Resistance, under the pretense of taking a child for a walk. One time, as we turned the corner from Avot Street to the park, a gust of wind picked me up off my feet. I flew up in the air like a kite, my hand held tightly by the strong hand of my father. He looked down at me and swung me forward with a laugh. His companion came around to take my other hand, and the two of them continued swinging me forward without slowing down or a moment's interruption in their conversation.

Every summer was spent at our cottage in Jurmala just as we had done before the war. Of course, we knew our letters were frequently opened and our telephones were monitored, and often the Nazi's security listened in on telephone conversations. At the beach I noticed that frequently a "friend" of Papa's, someone I had never met before, came out from the city in the evening to go for a swim and talk to Papa. They talked while walking on the beach and as they entered the water. Anna and I felt free, at the beach, to interrupt them and asked to be tossed in the air so we could come splashing down into the sea. They continued their conversation, without interruption, while we played. Person to person is the only way Papa communicated with others in the underground. If one of them was being spied upon, it looked like innocent summer activity.

In Riga, the dining room of our apartment was the largest of all the rooms. One evening my parents gave a dinner party that stands out in my memory. Anna and I received new dresses for the occasion, and the nurse fixed Anna's hair into ringlets with a hot iron. I thought she looked so beautiful. I wanted ringlets too, and I made a big fuss when I was told that my hair was not thick enough for ringlets. I made such a fuss that the nurse relented and curled my scrawny head of hair into ringlets as well. I looked in the mirror and realized I looked ridiculous with only two or three ringlets on either side of my face. I broke into tears and ran my fingers though my hair, destroying the sparse ringlets and leaving waves, which looked much better.

For years after that evening, every time I thought about it, I would feel very sorry for my bad behavior because the whole evening was so beautiful. There must have been seven or eight chairs down each side of the table and some at the ends. The silver and crystal glittered in the candlelight. There was a cluster of glasses at each place and beautiful flowers down the center. Mother wore a gown of shiny blue silk, the color of a cloudless sky at midday. I loved to touch the smooth soft silk. Anna and I were reminded to mind our manners as we greeted the guests with our parents.

I thought all the ladies looked so beautiful in their elegant gowns, and the men so handsome in their tuxedos under black coats and white scarves. During the dinner, Anna and I watched as the different courses were presented, being careful not to get in the way of the servers. The conversation was lively, filled with laughter and heartwarming toasts. After dessert, Papa said, "Well, it's time now for the men to come to the library and have a cigar."

The conversations and laughter subsided. I recall feeling tension rise as conversation ceased. Mother spoke up inviting the ladies to the parlor for coffee. When the guests departed from the dining room the French doors were closed and the servers got busy in the kitchen. Anna and I stayed behind, and alone in the room we started to imitate the ladies. We sat in chair after chair around the dining room table, pretending to talk ladylike. We sipped the wine that remained in all the glasses while commenting about the person who had sat there. There was white wine for the fish course, red for the meat course, and my favorite, a dessert wine. The more we drank, the more we laughed and came up with funny things the ladies might have said. I smile now recalling how silly we were and how much fun we had. Our cook and nanny were horrified when they came into the dining room to clean up. They spoiled our fun and sent us out of the room.

When the grownups finished their after-dinner coffee and cigars and emerged from their rooms into the foyer, I joined them, putting my arm around my mother's legs, enjoying the smooth, soft feel of her dress. She reminded me to curtsy nicely to the people as they left. Some of the guests talked about having their signature on an important document. Papa suggested they leave by twos or fours and not all at the same time. *Why is he saying they should leave by twos or fours, not all together?* I wondered. Even on such a beautiful evening, there was danger outside our door, I realized. That night, having stayed up so late, my legs hurt badly. Nurse put a pillow under them and said it was growing pains.

Many years later I learned that the document the Latvian leading men signed that evening was called *Memorandu*. It was delivered to the Roosevelt administration in America and the Churchill administration in England, by clandestine means my Father had arranged. In brief, that document declared that Latvia was occupied against her will by the Soviet Union and Nazi Germany and that Latvia, as a sovereign nation, an independent democracy, abhorred the atrocities committed by both.

Papa believed that a document signed by all these impressive Patriots could not be ignored by the Allies. He also believed that if all three Baltic countries presented a united front, it would carry more weight. They issued warnings to the free world that Stalin's Communist government was a present and serious danger to all freedom loving people, despite being considered an ally during the Second World War.

That document, signed in our apartment, helped in the ongoing struggle for Latvia's independence during the Cold War. It influenced future administrations in America not to recognize Latvia as a state of the Soviet Union. America continued to declare that Latvia was occupied territory for forty-five years. It also helped Latvians living in America, who spoke and worked against the Soviet Union's desire to have America release to them gold that democratic Latvia had stored at Fort Knox in the United States.

Papa had been an academic. After earning a law degree in Riga, he had studied in Paris at the Sorbonne, in Brussels, and in Berlin. International Law and Economics were his intellectual passion, but the War had diverted him into politics. How could he, the son of the first president of Democratic Latvia (whose roots were planted deep in Latvia's rich soil, dating back to the sixteenth century) how could he remain on the sidelines when Latvia was occupied and the freedom of her people oppressed?

In my mind's eye I can see a little suitcase, packed and placed by the door of our parent's bedroom in our Riga apartment. We had been told not to touch or move it. One time I saw Mother get upset when she went in the bedroom and it was not in its usual place. Our housekeeper said, "I am sorry, I am sorry. I was just letting the floor dry after mopping. I will return it to its place."

Mama's facial expression, when we walked into their bedroom, was definitely noteworthy; first surprise, and then fear, and then concern. There was something scary about that suitcase, I thought. Did Mama fear that Daddy had taken it and gone into hiding in a hurry while she was out? Our parents tried hard to protect us from the awful reality of war. They endeavored to provide a secure and happy home life, nevertheless, Anna and I intuited the danger of living in a war-torn country. We were instructed never to speak to strangers, the Nazi soldiers or anyone else about our family or life at home. We should not answer any questions, we shouldn't tell anyone who asks our name, where we live, who our parents are, or where they are.

One day, when I accompanied Mother to Schwartz Café, I went outside while she visited with a friend over a cup of coffee. I stood next to the bakery's window watching the people walking about and all the activity up-and-down the street. Looking at a horse-drawn carriage to my left, I was taken aback when a Nazi soldier came up to me, from the right and with a smile asked, "What is your name little girl? Would you like a piece of candy?" As he addressed me, I immediately bowed my head and looked down at his boots. Fear gripped my stomach and like a noose, attached itself to my throat. I slowly backed away from him to the door then quickly turned and went inside to stand beside my mother. She must have read the expression on my face. After looking at me, she looked out the window to where the soldier still stood looking inside. By the age of four I already understood German somewhat, thanks to Fraulein who had been our teacher.

Our apartment in Riga was a gathering place. It was not unusual for Papa to be visited by people with whom I was not familiar. They would go into his study, which was a long slender room, with three walls covered by bookshelves that reached up to the tall ceiling. At the far end, near the window, was my father's large desk. Along with the books and the desk there were a few comfortable chairs. Papa never considered it an interruption when Anna and I went into his office. We knew that behind the thousands of books, Papa hid a jar of candy. If we behaved, he would agree to find the candy jar. He would get up from the chair by the desk and walk round the room, remove a few books off the shelf and say, "Hmm, it's not there. Where could it be?" Then he would try a different shelf. We danced around him, saying, "Maybe on that shelf, or this one." Eventually he would "find" the jar of candy and let us choose a piece or two. Then he would say, "Now go on, but don't tell mother I gave you candy so close to dinnertime. She would scold me for spoiling your appetite for supper." We would giggle and leave him to work in peace.

I become a little spy quite by accident. One day, when Anna was having a piano lesson, I wandered into Papa's office with my dolly. I was not aware that several people had arrived to speak with him. I discovered an animated conversation in progress at the far end of the room. I knew it would be inappropriate for me to interrupt the grownups, so I squatted down on the floor to play quietly with my doll. Immediately and abruptly the conversation ceased. The sudden silence was audible. I looked up in time to see someone put a finger up to his lips and nod his head in my direction. After a moment of complete silence, with all heads turned to look at me, a lady present made the statement that commenced my spying career, "It's all right, she's much too young to understand." *I'm too young to understand what?* I thought to myself. I was always curious, so I took that statement as a challenge and recognized it as an opportunity. If I pretended to play with my doll in a make-believe game, I could eavesdrop and learn what the grownups were talking about. They had so many secrets. Being an inquisitive child, I wanted to know. I had noticed that when Anna was around my parents would often speak in different languages. They might switch to French, German, or Russian, but since I was "too young to understand," in my presence they could continue to talk in our native Latvian language. I had never paid much attention to their private conversations, but from now on I would be on high alert. The people in my father's office resumed their animated conversation. I was all ears. I learned that an attempt to kill Hitler was being planned. That would be good, I thought, then maybe these goose-stepping foreign soldiers would leave, but it was also frightening to think about my Papa being involved in something so dangerous. I understood that we were occupied by foreign Nazi troops. I saw them on the streets of Riga and had been instructed never to speak to them. I was not to tell them my name, I was not to respond at all if ever one of the soldiers tried to talk with me, and I was not to accept any candy if they offered it to me. As I continued to listen, I heard them mention Soviet soldiers as well.

Katrina and Anna in the playhouse at the cottage in Jurmala-1943

Chapter Four: *THE SOVIET OCCUPATION OF LATVIA - 1940*

Freedom, in any case, is only possible by constantly struggling for it. Albert Einstein

Anna told me a story about the Soviet occupation before the Nazis came. One night they had banged on our door so loudly it woke her up. "We were not in our beach house," Anna said. "It was an old, big house far away, I don't know where. Both of our grandmothers, Oma and Ama, and our grandfather, Apapa, were there that night, along with Auntie Marta, Aja and Jānis." "Where was Papa?" I asked. "The fathers were in hiding," Anna said. "The housekeeper must have opened the door to the banging. She was standing like a statue in the corner next to the front door when I came into the kitchen. The soldiers were coming right at me, so I had to back up to get out of their way. I fell backward into a pail of water used to mop the floor. I couldn't get out. I raised my arms, expecting one of the soldiers to help me get up from the pail I was stuck in, but they ignored me. With stern expressions they search the whole house." This took place approximately a month before my third birthday, and I have no recollection of the Soviet occupation.

Rumors and speculation of war were already raging in eastern Europe when I was born. Soon thereafter, in 1939, Stalin and Hitler concluded negotiations on a nonaggression pact, but a treaty entered into by two "devils" was not worth the paper it was printed on. The invasion of Latvia by Soviet Union forces in1940 inhibited every freedom we had known as a democratic people. They confiscated and occupied not only our summer cottage but also our grandfather's farm, Auci. The Communists did not believe in private ownership. By 1941 many of our political leaders had been arrested, killed, or simply disappeared. My father and many men like him, who had worked clandestinely to oppose the brutal Soviet occupation, went underground.

Papa had published an unauthorized newspaper exposing Soviet brutality. He wrote articles encouraging Latvian people not to participate in the election the Soviets staged. In that mock election everyone was required to go and vote - attendance would be recorded. There was only one candidate for each position, someone who would be a puppet of the Communist regime in Russia. There was no choice except to drop your vote in the box that said "yes" in support of their candidate or the box that said "no." Papa referred to that as a mock election in his newspaper. He did not dignify it with his participation. The nobility of his character would not permit him to remain on the sidelines in the struggle between good and evil, between freedom and oppression, between democracy and communism. He encouraged the Latvian people to be brave and steadfast and not give in to fear: fear of arrest if they did not go to vote, fear of arrest if they were seen voting "no" by the soldiers stationed at the voting boxes. He was definitely on the Soviet's blacklist. Stalin famously said, **"It does not matter who votes, it matters more who counts the votes."** Why would you go vote? Decisions made out of fear are usually not the right decisions.

Since our summer cottage in Jurmala had been taken over by the Soviets, we had rented a large, somewhat dilapidated fishermen's cottage near a small fishing village, on a very secluded stretch of the Baltic shore. One day in early June 1941 Mother took the train into Riga to visit her seamstress and pick up some dresses that were ready for Anna, who had outgrown her summer clothes, which I would inherit. As they chatted the seamstress expressed her concern about what was happening at the railroad yard. She said, "All the tracks are filled with train carriages and cattle cars. Soldiers are putting bars on windows and removing seats from passenger carriages. I'm afraid they are getting ready for a major deportation, don't you agree?" Mama certainly did agree. She did not go to our Riga apartment as planned, fearing arrest. Instead, she went to her parents' home to warn them and ask them to come back with her to the secluded cottage we were renting. On the way to their home, she stopped in every phone booth she saw and called as many relatives and friends as she could reach, to invite them to "come and play cards." That was the code the underground had for "you need to go into hiding."

One of my father's sisters was a music teacher. She was married, and her husband worked in the resistance with my dad. They had two little children. They decided that as long as her husband was in hiding, the KGB would not be bothered with her. After all, she was just a music teacher and mother of two youngsters. She stayed in her Riga apartment. On the night of June 14th, 1940 Soviet soldiers banged on their door and asked for her husband. She tried to explain to them, over their yelling, that she did not know his whereabouts. The loud voices awakened the children. Their mother told them to get their warm coats as they were going to a midnight picnic. She rushed around filling a basket with food and then grabbed some blankets. She didn't want the children to be frightened, therefore, she didn't tell them that they were being arrested. The Russian soldiers hurried them out of their apartment. Outside they were put in the back of an open truck. Other people were already in the truck looking gloomy. Whole families, many people who didn't even know there was an underground resistance movement, were arrested that night. My cousin, Valdis told me, "There was an older boy, in an Army uniform, sitting on the roof of the truck holding a big rifle. He had tears running down his cheeks." I thought that was very strange. I thought to myself, *"If I got to hold a rifle, I would be so proud, I sure wouldn't be crying!"*

At the time of his arrest, Valdis was only six years old. At the age of six he did not know that Latvian teenage boys were conscripted into the Soviet Army against their will, and that they were told if they didn't follow orders and shoot when told to, they would be shot. Little Valdis did not know that he was going to be locked in a train cattle car for a month-long journey to barren Siberia. On that long ride, locked in the carriage with a hole in the floor for a toilet, he would learn to live with hunger pains and fear. He would see an elderly woman die in that crowded freight car, grownups cry, and hard-hearted, soulless, soldiers push the dead person off the train then slam the sliding door shut as the grieving daughter tried to follow them out. She stood banging her fists on the locked door as the train once more started moving eastward, leaving her mother's body lying by the side of the railroad tracks. The forlorn daughter wept bitterly because she could not bury her mother. Valdis' mother and the other women surrounded her and held her while she cried. In their carriage there were only women and children. All of the men had been separated from their families and were taken to locked down slave labor camps. Valdis said he found a corner in the train car where he could peek at the outside world rushing past. Once in a while the trains slowed and pulled off the main track, and as it sat there waiting, it would become stifling hot in the windowless cattle car. Eventually, Valdis would see a passenger train with soldiers go past, heading west, transporting the men to the front lines in Europe.

When they finally reached the gulag, where their mother was assigned hard labor, to work off the sin of being a *bourgeois*, (that was what the Soviets call the upper class or people with higher education), they emerged from the train tired and dirty. They had to find their own lodging in what looked like a wilderness. A widow who lived alone in a one room hut finally offered them one corner of the room if the children would help with work and not be a nuisance. The little children had to sweep the dirt floor and collect firewood and kindling while their mother performed the labor assigned to her.

Communist Russian propaganda bragged about taking care of their workers — they provided a loaf of bread, a jug of milk, and some grain for a week. In the winter it was a block of frozen milk. During the summer and fall their mother asked them to gather nettles, which she would fry into pancakes to provide some vitamins to add to their bland diet. They didn't dare disobey her, no matter how much gathering the nettles stung their little hands and made their legs itch when they brushed against them.

Approximately ten years after being deported from Latvia to Siberia in the Soviet Union, Uncle Ringolds found them. Ringolds, one of Konstantin's older brothers, was a doctor and chief surgeon of the hospital in Jelgava. He remained in Latvia when the rest of the family escaped. As a doctor he felt responsible to protect his patients and his hospital with war raging around them. When bombs set a wing of his hospital aflame, he formed a bucket brigade with the help of many nurses. They fought the fire and saved the hospital. Foreign soldiers were brought into his hospital as well as the local population. He operated on anyone in need of a doctor; he did not discriminate. One man whose life he saved turned out to have been a Russian General. After the Nazis were defeated, this General came back to Jelgava and gave Uncle Ringolds an impressive medal for saving his life, and an officer's leather jacket.

Wearing that leather jacket with his distinguished medal on his chest, he took the train to Siberia in order to find his sister and her children and bring them home. He discovered, under the Communist Regime, government employees at every train station and transfer point demanding to know if he had papers and permission to travel. They all thought of themselves as little dictators, puffed up with the power of their government job. Uncle Ringolds addressed those little directors and clerks with the same bravado that he had observed the Soviet officers display when they addressed a man of lower rank. Wearing his impressive medal and his military leather jacket helped him cut through a mountain of red tape. He discovered that Valdis, age 17, was on his own, his mother was in a hospital and his sister was in a TB sanatorium. What had happened was that at the end of the Second World War the authorities who had distributed food to Aunt Maiga announced that food distribution would only be given to Soviet citizens. The "criminals" from foreign countries, who were living here, should not expect to receive any of the people's food. "They can come and apply for citizenship, and then they will qualify to receive food as before." Of course, Aunt Maiga did not want to become a citizen of the USSR. She tried to earn money to buy food anyway she could. She even pretended to be able to read people's palms because she had discovered that many Russian women were very superstitious. Life was very hard for them as well. Communism is an atheistic ideology. Communists taught that there was no God. "God is the opium for the masses dispensed by the rich and the powerful." We are created with a God shaped vacuum and will feel empty and lost seeking, searching for something, anything to fill that vacuum until we, at last, receive Him who is waiting for us. Without God we fear the future and become superstitious.

Despite Maiga's very best efforts to earn money for food for all three of them, she became very sick and was in danger of dying from starvation. Maiga felt that, to save her children's lives, she must sign the document to become a citizen of the USSR.

Ringolds found them all profoundly changed and unrecognizable. Valdis, after years of surviving the dehumanizing existence in Soviet Communist Siberia, told me that he had considered a stolen potato a great treat. He said he grabbed it and ate it raw. Approximately 70% of the 16,000 Latvian people who were deported on June 14, 1941 perished.

Chapter Five: *COULD I BE A KILLER AT THE AGE OF FIVE?*

"In that my conscience drove me, and in the end that is a man's duty," Field Marshal Helmuth Graf von Moltke.
"Shall I shoot?" (Hitler) Werner von Hoeften —
from *BONHOEFFER* by Eric Metaxas

Of course, when I was a little spy, in 1943 and '44, I didn't know all the details of Soviet brutality. But I sensed, from what I heard, that Soviet Communist soldiers were a great danger, just like our current occupiers, the Nazis. I decided, first we must get rid of the Nazis. I knew somehow that would be dangerous. I feared that my dad was involved with the group that wanted to kill Hitler. *I must think of a way to kill Hitler myself because I, as a child, would not be suspected*, I reasoned. After all, I was considered too young to understand what the adults were talking about. Therefore, it would be safer for me to try to accomplish the deed.

In one of my spying expeditions, I heard that many of the top Generals had been called back to Berlin for meetings with Hitler. *That's when I need to get to Berlin*, I thought to myself. Night after night, in my quiet, blacked out room I worked on my plot. One idea I developed was to put a bomb in my doll's stomach. Nobody would suspect her of being dangerous, and a little girl carrying a dolly would appear perfectly normal; no one would suspect that there was a bomb in her stomach. How could I get in where all the Generals were going to be meeting with Hitler? *Ah, after I get to Berlin*, I thought, *I could pretend to be the janitor's daughter, then go to the basement under their meeting room and leave my dolly to accomplish the deed*! If Hitler and his top Generals were dead, the War would shortly be over. At the time, I did not yet know that a few of the Generals had joined the plot to kill Hitler.

Oh, how my imagination worked! I wanted to save my dad, and I thought children could achieve what grown-ups could not. To the great disappointment of this budding spy, I later overheard that Hitler was not killed, but some of his top Generals had been sentenced to death. Hearing this I felt frustration that bordered on despair. I was convinced that I could have, would have killed him if I only had the means to accomplish it.

In Riga, the radio and news media declared the Nazis had saved us from the cruelty of Stalin's occupation. We should go back to living normal, happy lives and be thankful to the Fuhrer. In reality, we know we were occupied and always in danger. Any neighbor of ours, or even an acquaintance, could have been falsely accused of a terrible crime. The only way for them to make amends and save themselves was to become an informant to the SS. The SS wanted to know of anyone who criticized the Nazi occupation. Opposition was not tolerated and must be eliminated. One by one, all the dear people who helped Mama, came and told her they had been assigned full-time jobs to assist the German war machine. She tried to intervene, to no avail. She had hoped to keep at least one, a dear sweet lady who had been both nanny and cook. She came every day; we called her "Bubulits" affectionately. She was in tears when she told Mama she had to go work in an ammunition factory. The authorities recommended a new nanny Mama could hire. To say "no" would have raised suspicion. "How could I say no?" Mama said.

In 1944, the wailing of sirens by the Nazi emergency vehicles became more frequent day and night, and the bombs falling on our beautiful Riga had become intense with Soviet planes buzzing overhead. Our family moved out of the city to our summer cottage when frost still covered the ground, early in the spring of 1944. My sister and I were delighted — we could go outside without supervision, there was no sight of soldiers on our quiet lane — it felt safer to me. In Jurmala, our new nanny was busy helping mother plant a victory garden and doing other household chores. Anna and I were free to go outside by ourselves. Sometimes, when Mother had gone into Riga, we asked the new nanny to come play with us or read us a story. She said she didn't have time for that. It seemed to me that she never had time for us, she was always too tired or too busy with something else. "Mama, why do we have to have this new nanny?" Anna and I complained. We missed the dear people who had helped mother in Riga with washing and cleaning, especially our nanny who read stories to us. She even came inside our little playhouse in the garden. The new nanny was too fat to get through the door. Mamma said, "I was allowed to hire her, and I appreciate her help." Anna and I called her "Pancake" behind her back because she was very fat. We could tell our parents did not trust her or have the same affection for her as the dear people who had been assigned jobs helping the Nazi military. Why hadn't Pancake been assigned those jobs instead? Nevertheless, out there in our lovely beach resort, I felt far away from the noise and fear of the war. We were permitted to play games in our fenced yard and up in the sand dunes beyond. Beneath the tall pines that stood like sentinels between our house and the beach, protecting our home from the north winds that blow fiercely across the Baltic Sea in winter, Anna and I felt free and let our imaginations soar. We were not allowed to go down to the beach by ourselves. But there among the pines, we gathered varieties of mosses and pinecones and made our own little farms. Big pinecones became cows or horses, and little ones became sheep or chickens. When the wild strawberries ripened, and later blueberries, we would bring a basket with good intentions to pick them for dinner. Usually, I ate more than I brought home. Hours passed by quickly and the war seemed far away in these tranquil surroundings.

Father was not only the head of the Latvian underground resistance (his secret job), he was the Professor of International Law and Economics at the University of Latvia. Every morning he took the train into Riga for work. The best part of the day for me was when we walked to the train station to meet him in the evenings, welcoming him with hugs and stories of our day's adventures. Papa would give us his full attention, as if he had no cares in the world and our stories were the most important news of the day. At night I drifted off to sleep with fresh air blowing in the slightly open window. Even in our cottage at the beach black curtains had been installed, but at least Papa felt it was safe enough for Mama to open the window a crack. She always insisted that it was important for children to have fresh air. We drifted off to sleep with the wind singing a lullaby as it rustled the needles of the pine trees. I still cherish that sound. The meetings Papa conducted at our summer cottage usually took place on long walks along the beach. My sister and I were the excuse for these walks. Papa would say, "Children need fresh air," and Mama agreed wholeheartedly. He said it loud enough for Pancake to hear him, when she was helping clean up after dinner, or sometimes before dinner. Walking along the beach we would soon meet up with a colleague of Papa's, a gentleman who wanted to talk with him. I recall walking down the beach, running in and out of the surf, and then looking up and following Papa's gaze to the tree line. There I noticed, standing among the trees, looking to his right and left, was a gentleman wearing city clothes. It frightened me a bit. I looked up at Papa, but he just kept walking. After several minutes the man came out of the trees and walked along the beach to speak with Papa. Their hushed voices sounded grave. This was very detrimental for my spying career. It was much more difficult to eavesdrop while walking on the beach. Our parents made every effort to shield us from "adult concerns." One time, however, I overheard my dad giving instructions for travel to a young man, a student, who had joined us as we walked on the beach. I wondered where he was to go. During the Soviet occupation, all people were supposed to turn in their passports. Would he be trying to go to Germany to kill Hitler, like I wanted to do? Years later, I learned that one way my father communicated with the Allies was through carriers whom fishermen ferried to the Latvian Embassy in Sweden.

One early spring morning, while it was still dark, I was awakened from my peaceful sleep by dreadful rumbling noises coming through the slightly open window. They got louder and nearer, and then stopped in front of our cottage gate. My parents were awakened as well. I heard my mother, in an unfamiliar anxious voice, begging my dad to jump out the second-story window at the back of our cottage, where the first floor extends beyond the second floor, and go hide among the pines. I heard Papa run past our door to look out the window facing the beach. He must have seen that soldiers had already surrounded our home. He pleaded with Mama to open the door to stop the banging down below. He said, "They have surrounded the house. There are soldiers at the back. Give me time to get dressed and open the door before they break it down." Mama was crying, "The attic! Hide in the attic!" The attic could only be accessed through a hatch in the ceiling with a very, very tall ladder. Papa continued to urge Mama to go down and open the door to the banging that was increasingly getting louder and more violent. "You know they will search the whole house and they'll frighten the children." At last Mama ran down the stairs. No sooner had she descended that I heard the stomping of boots running up the stairs. They marched down the hall — their heavy boots with metal tips on the heel and toe sounded threatening. They marched into my parents' bedroom. A moment later my father, with two of those dreadful Nazi SS soldiers on either side of him, came into our bedroom to tell us good-bye. "Be good for Mama, I will be back," he said. Then the soldiers, with my Papa, stomped back down the steps and slammed the front door. I sat momentarily comatose in my bed, then got up and ran to the window to see if I could get a glimpse of Papa. The rumbling noise of all the vehicles and trucks, driving without any headlights on, receded into the early morning darkness. The cottage suddenly felt hollow. I was stunned and bewildered. I had not protected him. I comforted myself with Papa's last words, "I will be back!" I held onto those words as if they were gold bars or precious pearls. I repeated them in my mind whenever I started to worry about Papa. He was a man of his word, and if he said "I will be back," he will be back!

My mother was frantic. She opened our nanny's door and told her, and later us, that she was taking the first morning train into Riga. She was determined to obtain my dad's freedom. She needed to find someone at the university or someone in the occupation government to help. She asked for help from anyone and everyone she could possibly think of to get Papa free from that notorious prison, where people were tortured so inhumanely and brutally that screams could be heard out on the street, even from the deep dungeons.

"He is a professor of Law and Economics at the University of Latvia School of Law. He has worked with the University of Berlin, and after all, he is the son of Jānis Čakste the first President of Latvia! Couldn't he be released to house arrest?" Mama tried to stir up support for her campaign to have Papa released from prison. The charges against Papa had not been revealed. Mama did not know that the charge against Papa was espionage. The order for his arrest came from Berlin, from Hitler. Mama created such a stir that after several months the SS wanted to interrogate her.

That spring was very somber for Anna and me. We picked wild blueberries and strawberries, and sometimes helped with Mama's victory garden. As the end of June approached, Mama talked to us about going to our grandfather's farm, Auči, for Midsummers Night Celebration. It was traditional for the whole family to gather there for Jānis Name Day which coincided with Midsummers Night. Our grandfather, two uncles and two cousins were named "Jānis." The celebration of a "Names Day", is a tradition that most likely dates back to the 12th century. When grownups or children were Baptized, they received a new name, a Christian name, the name of a Biblical character, a martyr or a saint. Names Day was a more public celebration than a birthday, because everyone with a similar name was celebrated on that day. The cake was not as fancy, and the gift was smaller, but the flowers were just as abundant. The celebration of Midsummer's Night in Latvia dates back to before the Christian era and continues to be a special and joyful celebration, a celebration that gives special recognition to everyone named "Jānis." I had always looked forward to the joyful feast with the whole family who gathered together for several days at Auci.

The day we were to leave for Auči, Mother told us to come and sit down. She wanted to talk to us about something very serious. She said, "When we go to Auči, nobody is going to be talking about Papa's arrest, and you are not to mention it. Katrina, no loose lips, do you understand?" I was shocked but nodded my head obediently in a silent *yes*. She explained, "Oma, your grandmother, is very elderly, and has been traumatized by her daughter, Aunt Maiga's, arrest and deportation by the KGB. Therefore, the family thinks that hearing of her son's arrest by the SS would be too much stress for her to bear. So, do you understand, we must behave as if there is nothing wrong. You are not to talk about Papa's arrest! Do you understand?" she asked again. Anna and I nodded our heads to signify *yes*, but it hurt somewhere deep inside my chest that I couldn't' talk about my Papa.

My grandfather's farm, Auči, held so many happy memories for me. I recalled sitting on top of a tall horse in front of my Papa, with his arm securely holding me tightly around my waist. Anna sat behind Mama mounted on a beautiful bay horse, her arms around Mama's waist as we headed out on an adventure, riding around the farm. I liked horses very much; I liked the feel of their soft velvet noses when I held out my hand with a piece of an apple or carrot. Horseback riding was just one of the many fun family activities at Auči. Running around with our many cousins was so much fun, while climbing apple trees and picking apples in the orchard or visiting all the animals. One time when the nurse took all the cousins to feed the sheep, I found the littlest one, just like me, with whom to make friends. I gave it all the bread I had and snuggled the little lamb as I whispered to it that I would come back with some more the next day. The lamb sniffed my empty hands and then gave a big push to my stomach with her head. I fell over and she stood on top of me, demanding; I thought she was very ungrateful. Nurse had to come and help me up.

I was the youngest of Oma's grandchildren who slept in the loft of the tower. I had two cousins who were about a year younger, and they still slept in their parents' rooms. I treasure memories of happy Midsummer Night celebrations with the bonfires roaring brightly, food laid out for the taking, along with joyful singing and dancing. I always had to take a nap in the afternoon so I could stay up past midnight.

Papa had a great voice. With eyes sparkling, he invited all of us to sing along all the ancient "Ligo songs" which everyone knew from memory. When the musicians started playing folk dances, Mama and Papa joined in. Papa had looked so happy and Mama so graceful as they danced. Anna and I looked forward to our turn to dance with Papa; we knew he would come and dance us around the field. That was last year, last summer before the soldiers had taken Papa away. That was the first Midsummer's Night when I was considered old enough to sleep in the tower with all of Oma's grandchildren. That afternoon, when everyone was out of the house, I had gone in and up to the towers sleeping loft, and then back down the stairs to the second story where I counted the doors down the central hallway to make certain I could find my parents' room in the dark of night if I needed them. This Midsummer Night at the farm, Papa would not be there. I was not to talk about him. We were to act as if nothing was wrong. When Mama, Anna and I arrived at the beautiful farm all our aunts and uncles and cousins were there. Mama joined all the other ladies busy with food preparations. My sister ran off with some of our cousins. I stayed behind close to the house and watched all the activity. The men were preparing the bonfires — a large one on the grounds near the river, the other in a barrel on top of a tall pole. The pole was planted securely in the ground, with the roaring fire high up in the sky. It was a beautiful site. All was ready. Oma sat on the front porch looking up the long lane towards the road. She was invited to come down to the shore of the river for the festivities. But she sat there, not taking her eyes off the far away road. She said, "He will probably arrive on the next bus — let's just wait until then."

I sat down on the stoop of the doorway and pulled my dress over my knees down to my sandals and studied her. Her wavy silver hair was pulled back into a bun, her back was very straight. She looked regal. She was a very tall lady, the mother of nine children. She had lost her oldest son to the first World War, and one of her four daughters had been deported to slave labor camps by the USSR, along with two little grandchildren. No one had heard from them since they were locked in that cattle train car, as far as I knew. I don't think Oma had noticed me sitting slightly behind her on the stoop of the doorway studying her. She looked as if she was trying to bring my Papa home to her on the next bus by sheer willpower. We must have sat there for thirty minutes in silence. Finally, she became aware I was there, and she turned around to look at me. Her eyes seemed to question me. I looked straight back into her eyes, my head raised up, my lips pressed together lest the words I'm not supposed to utter slipped out. I wondered, *can she read in my eyes that which I am not allowed to verbalize, that my Papa, her son, is in prison and will not be coming tonight?* I secretly hoped that she could. I wanted her to be concerned for him; perhaps she could help bring him home. After the next bus came and went, Oma sighed deeply and said, "He has been detained in Riga; maybe he'll come later. Let's go down to the river where everybody is waiting for us."

My sixth birthday was in July. My mother tried to sound happy. She told me that her parents, whom we called Apap and Ama, were coming to stay with us and celebrate my birthday. But Papa wasn't going to be there, so I wasn't going to be happy about it. I loved Apap. His name was Antons Stipnieks. He was a businessman and banker. Whenever he came to visit us in Riga, he wore a morning suit or an evening formal suit, depending on the time of day. His suits were tailor-made to fit comfortably around his large stomach and slender legs. He wore a gold pocket watch in his vest pocket, the gold chain making an arch about his ample waste. As a businessman, he loved math. He would always ask us to do a multiplication or addition problems when he visited. Anna and I would usually get prepared, anticipating his question. When we got it right, he presented us with a silver dollar or *Lat*, as it was called in Latvia.

At the seaside in Jurmala he would wear a comfortable summer suit, as my birthday table was set outside in the garden. Nanny helped me dress in one of Anna's old dresses — it had been sewn from imported silk before the war. It was pink with the shiny side of the silk on the inside. It felt so smooth next to my skin. Even at that young age I knew my dress was fancier than Anna's new cotton one, so I did not mind wearing a hand-me-down. When I went outside, I twirled around happily, seeing the pink silk spread out around me like an open umbrella. Then I saw my birthday chair, decorated with all white flowers. My sister's birthday chair had been so colorful, I recalled. In February, they used store-bought flowers to decorate the chair for the birthday girl who sat like a princess on a throne surrounded with bright colored blossoms. I thought her chair had been much more beautiful and colorful. My chair was decorated with flowering branches from our own garden. With a pout on my face, I decided not to enjoy myself. I sat down in my chair arms folded across my chest. Then the wonderful fragrance of the blossom's enfolded me and melted away my discontent and jealousy. My grandparents' loving presence brightening the evening as well. They had brought a delicious cake from Riga, and I was happy that they were spending the night. I was also happy that Nanny Pancake would be leaving us for a day off after cleaning up. In the morning I ran downstairs and out the open back door where I discovered Apap and Mama digging deep trenches in our garden. Many of our valuables, silverware, candlesticks, and even dishes were being buried in the ground. "Just in case the soldiers come to our house," Mama said. "And you must not talk about it. Don't tell anyone what we have done, not even Nanny, if she asks, where these dishes are. Do you understand?" *Yes, yes I know about the danger of "loose lips,"* I thought. In wartime there were so many secrets and far too many things that we were not allowed to talk about.

As summer turned to fall and the leaves on the trees started to turn colors of gold, orange, and red; we received the devastating news that Papa was being transferred to a concentration camp in Germany. Even though, at the time, I did not know the brutality of concentration camps, a shiver went down my spine. Given my youth, all that I feared was that my father was being taken far away from us. Mama was visibly upset after getting the news. It wasn't in her nature to show emotions, much less crumble on the floor in distress or ever cry. Instead, with lips quivering, she rushed around like a tornado prepared a little suitcase with some warm clothes and food for him; then she dashed out the door to take it to her father who had agreed to deliver it to her beloved husband. This was necessary because the SS suspected her of involvement in anti-Nazi resistance work, so it was not safe for her to say goodbye to Papa. But she walked with her father as far as it was safe for her to do so, and then she stood in the shadows only able to watch from afar. It's then she witnessed her father forcefully breaking through a column of SS soldiers to give the life-saving suitcase to her husband. With tears running down her cheeks she noticed a brief exchange between the two most important men in her life. She later learned that in that brief second our Papa implored Apap, "Tell Anastajia to save our children." Then the soldiers pushed our seventy-three-year-old, very dignified grandfather, out of the way. She heard Papa call after him, "Please give her red roses for me!"

My Uncle, the Rev. Jānis Terins, Dean of Doma Cathedral, wearing his clericals, was not manhandled by SS Guards as he walked beside the column of guards the last part of their march to the ship. He spoke loudly so Papa could hear and was able to reach past a couple of a SS soldiers and hand him a package of cigarettes. My Dad was not a smoker but what Uncle Terins had in mind was that Papa could exchange cigarettes for food, as most of the soldiers were smokers. It was obvious to everyone that Papa had already lost an awful lot of weight.

After Papa had been taken from us and sent to a faraway prison, the sun seemed to have stopped shining on our dear cottage, and the sense of stability and joy we used to enjoy was clouded over. Mama never smiled anymore and was often gone. Whenever she was at home, she and Nanny were busy working in the garden harvesting fruit and vegetables. They boiled glass jars, which then they filled with strawberry, blueberry, and raspberry jam as well as peas, green beans, and cucumbers, for the anticipated food shortage. Anna and I were allowed to help pick berries or shell peas, but mostly we were told not to get underfoot.

In the late fall, the leaves had all fallen, leaving the trees as bare and forlorn as my heart. Now even in this once tranquil beach resort the thunder of bombs could be heard more frequently and loudly, causing a shiver down my spine. That's when we learned we had to escape and to depart from our dearly loved summer cottage, our grandparents, and our country.

Papa, Katrina, and Anna
1943

Chapter Six: *HEAVEN IS NEAR*

"Go out into the darkness and put your hand into the Hand of God. That shall be to you better than light and safer than a known way." From a poem by Minnie Louise Haskins.

One evening when our Nanny had been given the day off, Anna and I discovered Mama packing and unpacking and packing again one little suitcase, trying to decide what was most important to take with her. Tears were running down her cheeks, then she wiped her cheeks with the back off her hand and sent us back to bed without explanation. In the morning our uncle, who we called Aucu Uncle, arrived to escort us to the train station. We were given a hearty breakfast and told to dress in two dresses and a sweater — no questions asked. Then I had to shove my arms into my coat. I felt like a stuffed sausage! Under normal circumstances I would have complained bitterly if a sleeve of my dress got jammed up in my coat sleeve, but these were not normal circumstances, and I instinctively knew this was not the time to complain. We had to escape from the bombs and the foreign soldiers, but to where? My questions remained unspoken; there was no time. I bit my lower lip and picked up the backpack I was to carry, and off we went to the train station. At the train station I heard adults talking about the devastation and the tragic destruction of Riga by the bombs. I wondered where are we to go? My questions were burning inside of me, but I realized there was no time; I must just do what I'm told to do, and no questions asked, during this dark, scary time.

The underground had arranged for an express train from Riga, to slow down and pick up mail at our little beach resort train stop. As the train slowed, doors opened and my uncle tossed me onto the train, my sister was tossed into the next carriage, and then my mother along with her suitcase jumped in last. I sat on the floor, looking up at the strangers who looked as surprised as I did. I didn't move. I sat there in full confidence that Mama would soon come. It wasn't long until I saw her coming through the train carriages collecting her children and belongings. The train picked up speed, heading towards a fishing village in the most western part of Latvia.

In Ventspils, we were taken to a little apartment. One aunt, an uncle, and cousins were already there. Adults had to talk privately again, so my sister and I were asked to leave the room. We wandered out the door of the apartment and downstairs to the street. We looked up and down that little street. Not seeing any soldiers, we felt quite safe and happy to be outside. A man dressed all in white with a big white hat came weaving his way down the sidewalk towards us. *What fun*, I thought, *a clown has come to entertain us*. We started laughing and I pushed him playfully one way, trying to tickle his side, then my sister pushed him the other way. He swung his arms around in a circle batting us away. We thought he was playing with us. Our game did not last long, because our laughter and his incoherent loud voice were heard up on the second floor. We were sternly reprimanded for harassing that intoxicated baker!

I don't recall how we all slept in that little place that night, but the next day we were packed into a truck and driven to a farm. As soon as we arrived, we were rushed into the barn; we had no time to look around. A woman, I presumed was the farmer's wife, hurried us into the barn. "A lookout has spotted German soldiers nearby, so you have to hide quickly," she said anxiously. In the barn I had to climb up a ladder to the hayloft. I was told to lie down on a bed of hay and then hay was piled up on top of me. After I was covered from head to toe in a cocoon of hay, I was instructed to lie absolutely still. I was told that no sound, no movement was to be heard. The floorboards of the hayloft were separated just enough so that, after I cleared away some hay near my face, I could look down towards the barn door. Always curious I wanted to see what was going on down below. A few minutes after absolute silence had settled over the barn, it was interrupted by voices. The same lady was casually chatting in German to a soldier. Now her voice sounded relaxed and casual. As their voices got louder and clearer fear was rising in me, I thought, *they must be coming to the barn.* Just a few minutes earlier, the farmer's wife had been so officious. Now she sounded so jolly, relaxed, and casual. I understood German a little, and I was thankful that my parents had employed teachers to come to our Riga apartment. Hiding under the hay I was glad I could understand some of what the farmer's wife was saying. "Ja ja, we milked this morning. Come on in the barn

I'll give you some fresh milk." To my horror, I saw the dreaded Nazi soldier right there in the barn beneath me. He was turning his head from left to right, looking around the barn. Was he going to start searching the barn? At that thought I stopped breathing in case each breath was causing the hay to rustle loud enough to be heard down below. That was not a good idea, however, because after holding my breath for a while I had to draw in a larger breath, and my torso lifted the hay even more. I was scared to death that the soldier may have noticed. He walked deeper into the barn and disappeared from my view. The lady continued to talk nonstop while dipping out some milk from the milk cans that stood just inside the barn door. When she raised up, she offered him the cup of milk and invited him to go to the house "for something stronger." She knew the soldiers must have seen the truck arrive. "Some friends of mine came out from town to visit me, would you like to meet them?" she asked. They walked out of the barn and their voices faded away. I exhaled in the relief.

I heard later that my mother and the other young women were in the farmhouse. The ladies had mixed medical grade, ninety-five proof alcohol with honey and juices — quite a potent cocktail to offer the soldiers. As night approached, it started to drizzle outside. The German soldiers were enjoying the cocktails and showed no interest in returning to their job of patrolling the forest in search of defectors. Just to be sure it was safe to leave, the ladies had asked the soldiers if they would like to take a walk down to the beach, but they had fallen asleep. Once they were convinced that the soldiers would not stir, they determined that it was safe for us to make our way through the woods to the beach.

Under the hay cocoon, I had drifted off to sleep. A gentle tapping on my shoulder awakened me. Peeking through the floorboard, as I raised up on all fours, I could see nothing but absolute blackness. The hay was brushed off my back, without a word exchanged Mother took my hand and guided me back to the ladder. Quietly we descended the ladder and then the backpack was placed on my back. My uncle took my hand in his and we started walking as Mother turned back and picked up her suitcase. Heavy clouds covered the night sky. It was so black I could not see my hand in front of my face. It was a perfect night for our escape. My uncle and I started walking quickly towards the woods, an uncle, aunt, cousins, and my Mother, carrying the little suitcase and holding Anna's hand, followed close behind. After we reached the tree-line we slowed our pace. Silently and carefully, we made our way through the dark forest. My uncle was very alert, I could feel him constantly turning his head, peering into the darkness as we made our way forward without making a sound. Then suddenly he stopped and motioned for everyone to squat down. Out in the darkness, among the trees, I saw dark shadows, swaying, moving noiselessly. They were coming in our direction. *Are they soldiers? Did they see us?* The tension was palpable. I could feel my heart beating in my throat as they approached, looking like black trees walking. They had seen us, it was clear - they were coming toward us. Seconds seemed like hours. To my great relief, we soon knew. They were not soldiers; it was a doctor and his family. They had gotten word of our escape and took the great risk of walking to the beach, attempting to join us. My uncle didn't talk to them, nor did they say anything. No one spoke, not a word was exchanged. It would've been too dangerous for us to send them back, so they had to come along.

During those anxious moments of not knowing if we were about to be discovered and arrested by soldiers, my hand had slipped out of my uncle's, and I stepped off the path and found myself sliding down into a deep hole. I tried to push up, but I couldn't. A root from a tree must have caught my backpack. Stuck in the hole up to my eyeballs, I watched as our group resumed walking one by one, their legs passing me just out of reach. I didn't make a sound. I did not want to endanger our party by calling for help. Suddenly I couldn't see the silhouetted legs anymore — all was deep black before my eyes, and then the heavy weight of a foot pressed down on my shoulder. I reached up and a familiar hand grasped mine. It was my Mother. She too had slipped off the path. At the feel of her hand, great relief welled up inside of me. I wanted to hug her and hold her and tell her how glad I was that she discovered me; but showing her that she could trust me to remain silent was more important. We said nothing to each other as she freed me and pulled me out. We resumed walking silently, Mama holding my hand tightly, with my sister on her right side holding on to the handle of the little suitcase Mama carried.

When we arrived at the beach, people talked in hush voices to one another. We were standing on top of a very steep sandbank. The shoreline looked to me to be fifteen or twenty feet below us. I was told to sit and slide down the sand to the shore, which to me sounded terrifying. Anna whispered "it will be fun". I did not agree, nevertheless, gritting my teeth, swallowing my fear, I sat down on the edge and immediately found myself descending faster and faster, at a steep angle, towards the beach below. Fear was replaced with momentary joy. I discovered that Anna was right — I did not need to be afraid, sliding down was really a lot of fun. There was no time to linger, however, we had to board rowboats and were told, "Sound carries across the water, even a whisper, therefore, not a word, not a sneeze is to be uttered." I was picked up and placed in the bow of the first boat. Then I saw Anna and Mama climb in with a few others. Two men took the oars, and with their rhythmic *splash, splash*, we moved out across the rolling waves of the Baltic Sea toward the black, invisible horizon. I kept my eyes fixed on the shoreline, as if my eyes could hold it close. We moved farther and farther away from Latvia and all that was familiar to me. Even though the night was black as pitch, the white sand of the beach was visible and seemed to shimmer. The line of shimmering sand became thinner and thinner as we rowed farther out across the rolling waves. My eyes wanted to hold on to the shoreline — the shoreline of my land, where my home was, where my Papa said he would come back to me. How will he find us now that we are not there?

I was surprised when the oarsmen pulled up beside a tall fishing vessel. Heads appeared, leaning over the deck. They dropped a fishnet over the side and one of them climbed part way down. One of the oarsmen climbed part way up from the rowboat, which rode the waves up and down beside the much taller fishing vessel. The other oarsman, who was still in the rowboat, picked me up and lifted me high, over his head. Up I went quickly from hand to hand until I was on board. No one had spoken a word. I was carried across the wooden deck, the clop, clop of a man's footsteps the only sound to be heard. Then he lifted me across a plank, that I perceived to be the other side of the boat, and started to drop me. Beneath me I heard the waves breaking against the side of the boat. I grabbed for his arms. Looking down I could see nothing but black. *He is dropping me in the sea*, I thought. I grabbed his jacket, and I tried to hold onto his arms, but he kept pulling my hands away so that he could drop me. I couldn't see his face. It was so dark, and he said nothing while we struggled with each other. I thought, *that because I had fallen into that hole in the woods, I had become a liability to the group and could endanger this escape. Was that why he had decided to throw me overboard*? I was fighting for my life. *I am about to die*, I thought. I didn't know how to swim, and I did not want to drown in the cold, dark sea. I started to scream at the top of my lungs. My Father was far away in a Nazi prison, he couldn't help me. My Mother was still in the rowboat on the other side. Could she hear me? I was all alone with no one to help me, fighting with all the strength my six-year-old body could muster. I tried to grab onto his sleeve, the collar and his jacket, trying to save myself from a big strong man who was trying to drop me in the sea. **Finally, I was at the end of all hope and depleted of all strength. I knew I could not save myself, and there was no one to help me. I cried out, "God help. Jesus save me!" I yelled it as loud as I could, "Jesus save me."** At that moment, the moment of my greatest need, fear, and helplessness, our loving Heavenly Father parted the curtains between the seen and the unseen world. **I saw a vision from heaven. I was enfolded in light, and before me was a face as bright as the sun, his arms open to me. From his eyes, rays of love showered me.** His clothes were dazzling white, his face was too bright to discern any features. His eyes — oh, those eyes! They shone brilliantly with joy and love. His beauty was indescribable, iridescent! He looked at me, no he looked *into* me it seemed. He knew me. I could tell he knew everything about me. That was a little frightening, and a shiver went down my spine. Every nasty thought laid bare, every jealous impulse I had ever had he seemed to know. Yet he "*helloed*" me with pure love. I felt ashamed for having been jealous of my sister. I could tell he saw that, but still he welcomed me with love and joy. I felt bathed in his love and I wanted to go to him, to be with him and never leave his presence. Death no longer frightened me. I ceased to fight my tormentor. I wanted to fall into those loving, open arms and be with him forever, even if that meant I had to first drown in that once terrifying sea. I was no longer afraid. I let go. Down, down I fell! To my surprise I didn't land in the cold, dark water, like I had thought I would. I landed in a fishnet. That was not where I wanted to be. I longed for him, to be held in those wonderful loving, waiting arms. Instead, I lay in the net that felt like a hammock, and I was back in familiar blackness, disappointed and sad. The waves continued to pound against the side of the boat. Once I oriented myself to my surroundings, I realized I was lying on a fishnet down in the cargo hole. I knew I was temporarily safe, and my tired legs could rest, but I was so disappointed. Soon other people were lowered down to lie beside me. I didn't know if one of them was my sister. It was too dark to recognize anyone, and no one said a word. When everyone was on board, and the sound of footsteps ceased, the fishing vessel began to steam westward, the motor chugging rhythmically. I relaxed and started to drift off to sleep, thinking about Jesus, wondering if I had seen Him or was it an angel? ***No, it had to be Jesus, because he knew my thoughts, he could hear them*****, I concluded. One thing I knew for sure, Heaven was beautiful, and God really sees us even on the blackest night**.

"A German destroyer is steaming in our direction," a male voice above me whispered. That was followed by the rustling of bodies pressing against each other and tension that was palpable. Our vessel changed direction with cranking noises breaking the silence. We were heading south, in the direction of Germany, I surmised. Minutes seemed like hours. I saw a bright light move across the hatch above me. No one was up on the deck except the fisherman. After a while, it became evident that the destroyer was not coming to search our fishing vessel; it continued north. A collective sigh of relief was exhaled by all when they told us "all clear." With cranking noises our boat changed directions once more, heading westward towards safety in Sweden.

I continue to ponder the experience I had. Could God protect our boat from being seen by the Nazis? He was real to me now. I could talk to him in my thoughts because I had seen that He could hear them. I had known enough about Him to call to Him, to call for help, but had I really expected Him to help? I don't know. I suppose in that moment, I must have understood that he could help. Now I knew He is real and present. *He really is*. That revelation brought a flutter of joy in me, even in that very dark time.

I thought about how to tell my mother. I wanted to tell her what had happened. But how could I describe it? Then I remembered that, because I was so young, adults didn't take what I said seriously. What would her reaction be? How could I describe an experience so profound to make her believe me? It was too important to be taken lightly, as adults tend to do with what children tell them. If she dismissed it or minimized this in any way, I couldn't take it. On second thought, I decided this would remain my secret — our secret. If God want to tell her, he could. I would not share my experience with anyone.

The next day we safely docked at the island of Gotland, a Swedish Island in the Baltic Sea.

Katrina Čakste
In Sweden
Wearing a
Latvian National
Costume
1947

Chapter Seven: *EXILED IN SWEDEN - 1944*

"Our native soil draws all of us, but I know not what sweetness, and never allows us to forget," by Publius Ovidius Naso
The Poem of Exile: Tristia and the Black Sea Letters

When the fishermen docked at Gotland, we exhaled in relief and jubilation. The adults were hugging each other with hearty claps on the back. Soon we were greeted by Swedish "authorities" who took us for medical examinations. Because we came from a warzone, all of us had to be sanitized in showers with harsh soap that turned the grey hair of one lady, pink and caused a burning sensation on my scalp. Then we were examined by medics and received many shots. It was all very distressing to me. The jubilation of the grownups, when we landed on the shores of Sweden, had pulled me in to share their relief. Now the relief turned to despair. I had survived foreign soldiers searching for us and the thunder of exploding bombs, and the feeling of being displaced mingled with fear accosted me. I started to cry. Mama tried to help me understand that the Swedish authorities didn't want people bringing diseases to their population from a country beset by war. But I could not hold the tears back anymore. The suppressed fear and loss that had been a heavy weight in the pit of my stomach finally wanted release. Even though I bit my lip and tried to be brave, the tears kept coming. The clothes we wore, as well as everything we had brought with us, had to be disinfected. This didn't feel like safety and freedom to me. That first night we slept on mats in a large stone church. The next morning Mama made me bathe in the freezing cold sea. She poured water over my head to wash off the chemicals. When our belongings were returned to us, we discovered Mama's mink coat, after being disinfected, was unusable. Instead of throwing it away, she salvaged the good parts of the fur. For the next forty years she made lots of collars for our wool coats and dresses. After what seemed to me a dreadful time in Gotland, we were transferred to a resort that was closed for the winter.

At last, I felt safe and grateful to the Swedish Crown for hosting us. Sweden was neutral, so it was a great risk to their neutrality and a sacrifice for them to shelter refugees from a country occupied by waring powers. Whenever the adults gathered in the living room of the lodge and started a serious, quiet conversation, I resumed my spying techniques, sometimes hiding behind draperies to listen. I wanted to know when the war would be over, when Papa would be free, and when I could return home. One day, to my surprise, my mother and the other adults were not discussing the war, they were discussing my sister. Anna had a stomach ache and was in bed. I heard the Latvian doctor say that she needed an operation — she had appendicitis. Here we were in the middle of a forest, far away from a major town, in a foreign land, and my sister needed an operation. *"Dear Jesus, you can see Anna; oh, please help her, Mama looks so upset,"* I whispered, squatting behind the curtain. When an ambulance came, I ran outside to wave goodbye to my sister. I didn't even mind being left behind because I was glad Mama was allowed to go. I watched her get in the ambulance with Anna and drive off. I went back inside, found a secluded corner to hide in and talk to God. I really was glad that Mama had been able to go with Anna, but now I felt so all alone in this unfamiliar place, I realized I didn't even know where I was. It was such a comfort to talk to God, to know He could hear my thoughts and see us. I hoped Anna would get to see Jesus the way I had when I was in trouble. Then I wouldn't have to keep this secret all to myself.

In Latvia, all windows had to have blackout curtains so no light would be visible from the street or from bombers in the sky. All lampposts on street corners stayed dark as well. Here in Sweden, the lampposts on the streets shone brightly, and lights could be seen in all the windows. That was wonderful since this far north, night falls early in the afternoon, in the fall, and wintertime.

After my sister had recovered from her surgery, one afternoon Mama took both of us out for a walk. Off in the distance, I saw a moving bright light coming toward us. *Is that the light of Christ I saw on the fishing vessel?* I wondered. *I am not going to wait for him to come to me.* I started to run toward the light as fast as I could. My mother grabbed my arm. I pulled away from her. I was so excited to see him again, and with my whole being I wanted to run to him, to run toward the approaching light. I didn't want Mama to stop me, she was holding on to me so tightly and I was trying so hard to pull free that we lost our balance and fell down. Both of us ended up on the ground, with Mama on top of me. Then the bright light of a car drove past. I felt devastated, deeply disappointed, foolish, and embarrassed. Heartbroken, I cried. Mama asked me "what got into you, why were you trying to run into the street? I couldn't tell Mama why I had tried to run — at a car. I felt so foolish. In my mind, I heard the words, "*Not that way.*" The words sounded stern, not critical but stern, somehow, and I knew this was definitive. Those words came to me very clearly and with a deeper understanding in my inner being that I had to wait on the Lord. He acts when He acts. He is sovereign. Since I had not told my mother about the experience I had on the fishing vessel with Jesus, I could not explain to her why I had tried so hard to run at a car. My experience was too important, and God was as real to me as my mother was. I cried and did not try to explain myself. I had mistaken the lights of an oncoming car to be the light of the glory of the Lord coming back to me. I felt so stupid, and I cried with disappointment and longing to see him again. I said nothing when Mama asked again what got into me. The words I had heard in my head as I lay on the ground were stern, not judgmental, but strong and clear — *Not that way*! I had much to learn I realized, and I longed for His presence. The memory of his love soothed my disappointment. The reason for my potentially serious mistake could not be shared with Mama. Not then. I had to keep my secret. I loved and longed for more understanding of God.

Chapter Eight: *IN THE SHADOW OF DEATH - 1945*

"The death of a beloved is an amputation."
C.S. Lewis, A Grief Observed

With the winter thaw and the first blooms of spring, our hopes of seeing Papa again blossomed as well. The war was coming to an end. We heard that survivors from concentration camps were in dreadful shape, skeletal and sick and needed to be taken to hospitals in Denmark. We anxiously waited for news that Papa was among them. Then one day news arrived. *What was happening?* I wondered in shock and my stomach began to churn with anxiety. My strong, fearless, Mother was falling down? Weeping out loud? A gut-wrenching wail erupted from the depth of her being, followed by great, ragged sobs. Father's sisters, our aunts, surrounded Mama, trying to support her when her feet slipped out from under her. The aunts took her to the room next door, leaving Anna and me alone. We embraced each other. Tears welled up in my eyes, and I could hear Anna crying quietly. Without having been told, we surmised what news mother had received, the news we dreaded — that our father had not survived. I started to think, *This is too terrible! He told us he would be back. Maybe it isn't true? Could he have escaped and hidden away somewhere? Are they sure?*

My Dad was a man of his word. If he said he would return, he would try every way humanly possible to come back to us. I wanted to hold onto hope that today's news was a mistake. We had no one to tell us what happened, no one to comfort us. Grief takes many forms, and denial is just one of them. I think I entered a deep inward fog, drawing into myself, living in the memories of my father and home, determined not to forget any feature of his face or the feel of his hand on my forehead. I recalled his cool hand soothing my headache when I had a fever. When I heard a song, my father sang as he taught me to dance, I reached up as if he could hold my hands in his larger, stronger ones and recalled that he would tell me to watch his feet and move mine with his. Then he would start singing the melody, counting "1-2-3, 1-2-3" to the tune of a waltz and I, looking down at his big feet, would follow along counting "1-2-3, 1-2-3" with him. When at last I got it right, he praised me and started to sing the words instead of the numbers and we danced on for a while. How I loved his laughter! It was like a waterfall, gushing forth, filling the room with joy. His presence brought sunshine even into cloudy days. His death meant I would never see him again — it is so permanent. That dreadful black, frightening night of our escape, when God had allowed me to see beyond the veil, to see His indescribable beauty, purity, and love, I wondered, *Is Papa there now?* Mama, Anna, and I were alive, but living the coming days under the darkness of grief, in the shadow of his death, was as if a pall covered us. Loneliness engulfed me. We were a fatherless, homeless, stateless threesome. We couldn't return to Latvia because of the threat of being deported to Siberia in a cattle car by the Communists, like my aunt and our two little cousins. Amid the grief, however, I didn't think much about tomorrow, only the present day. I tried to be still and quiet and not add to my Mother's heartache. We were to attend a memorial service. My sister and I were to dress in dark blue matching dresses with white lace collars and cuffs. Mama, dressed all in black, sternly informed us we must sit very still when we arrived at the service, and to me she added, "Katrina, do not fidget!" We sat in the front row and listened to all the wonderful things people were saying about my father. "He was a champion of the Latvian people, his work for liberty and democracy must continue as an example for future generations." "His sacrifice must never be forgotten." "He was a hero in the concentration camp as well," they had heard from a survivor in the hospital in Denmark. In the barracks with other Latvian political prisoners, when some felt unable to go on living because of being overworked, starving, sick and cold, Papa had persuaded them to get on their feet, move and sing. Singing Latvian folk songs, which they all knew by heart, revived them to endure one more day - one more day. From "spying" I had learned that Papa was involved in dangerous work on behalf of Latvia's freedom, but now I was hearing more about it. I had not been able to kill Hitler, but Hitler had caused the death of my father. Sitting in the front row, beside my sister, I felt anger bubble up through my grief.

I wished I could hear Papa's rich, baritone voice once more. I missed him so much. Somehow it was comforting to know that so many other people, strangers to me, also missed my Papa a great deal. The following week there was another memorial service. My white collar was rinsed out, ironed, and reattached to the dress, and off we went. Even though I was glad that so many other people missed him almost as much as I did, it was hard to sit there, not fidget, and swallow the tears on the verge of flowing down my cheeks. My mother was stoic, stone-faced in her black dress, her face covered by a black veil, and I did not want to be a burden to her.

After all the services and lovely words spoken about my father, we found ourselves alone, the three of us. My cousins with their moms and dads became resigned to the present reality and started making plans for a new life. The three of us were invited by a kind Swedish lady to spend the summer at her guest cottage, located behind her home in a lovely resort village of Sigtuna. In exchange for her hospitality my mother would help her around the house and in her extensive garden. She was an elderly widow and to some extent could identify with my mother's sorrow. There was a sewing machine available. Mama figured she had observed so many seamstresses that it shouldn't be too hard to try her hand at sewing, and soon she presented us with simple little summer frocks for outside playtime. The house was built on a hillside, and beyond the garden stood a forest to explore. One day Anna and I discovered a large rock, at least eight or nine feet high, with one shiny side sloping down at a step angle. It made a perfect slide. We slid on our bottoms a few times and then decided to run back to the house to see if we could find some cardboard boxes to use as a sled. Dragging the flattened boxes back to our lovely boulder, we ran up and slid down again and again. Suddenly, I felt a burning sensation on the skin of my bottom as I slid down. *Oh no! How could that have happened?* I thought. Yes indeed — the rock had worn a hole in the cardboard and my bloomers. I went home downcast. When Mama saw our expression, she asked what happened. I turned around and bent over, feeling so sad. I had ruined the new bloomers she had sewn for me. Looking up at her I saw that she was covering her mouth with her hand, stifling laughter at seeing two very pink buttock cheeks exposed! I was embarrassed but also happy to see her smile. She was very busy with gardening and cleaning and cooking. We helped her pick berries to make jams for our hostess, who was kind enough to teach Mama Swedish as they worked together. They had French as a common language.

Perhaps you've heard it is said that things happen in threes. One day when my mother was in the outhouse, as that little cottage did not have indoor plumbing, we heard a loud shriek, the door of the outhouse flew open, and my mother shot out of there with her britches around her knees! She had surprised a wasp who did not want to share the "throne" with her. After recovering from that dreadful encounter, she went back to stir her jam which was gently bubbling on the stove. My sister and I went back to chasing each other around the yard. Anna decided to run into the house to hide and dashed through the little galley kitchen. She ran into Mama, jarring her arm, and some of the boiling jam sloshed out and landed on my sister's foot. Another big yell from Mama and Anna. Mama quickly reached down and took off my sister's shoe and sock. As the sock was removed, I was horrified to see the skin came with it — the burn was so severe. I was immediately scolded and sent outside.

I felt terrible, was it my fault that Anna got burnt? I shouldn't have chased her, I thought feeling guilty. What could I do, to take my mind off my sister's pain? I went to play on the railing of the stone steps that descended to the front of the main house and the lower part of the garden. Hanging from the bar by my knees and twirling around like a gymnast, distracted from our troubles I was feeling better. Suddenly I slipped and fell headfirst on to the rocks below. Head wounds tend to bleed profusely! Picking myself up with blood running down my face, crying I ran back to the wee cottage to tell Mama. A doctor had been summoned to examine my sister's foot. He looked at my head and told my mother not to worry about me, it was a surface cut. I said to him, "What about my mother's bottom? She got stung by a wasp today." Mother's cheeks reddened as she concentrated on Anna's seriously burned foot. The doctor smiled as he said, "My, my, you have had quite a day."

Mama was accustomed to having a staff look after us fulltime. She had a live-in nanny, a cook, a housekeeper, and someone who came in to do the washing. The washing in Latvia was done with great big pots used to boil the sheets on the stove, after which two women would wring out the sheets, twisting them as dry as possible, then stretching and hanging them outside or in the drying room. Now Mama had no one to help her. She was mother, nursemaid, cook, housekeeper, laundress, and even seamstress.

As fall approached Mama's Swedish language skill was greatly improved, and Anna and I had learned enough of this new language so that we would be able to get along in school. We had never been in an organized school before — it was considered too dangerous living under occupation in a war-torn country. Mama had moved a desk into the nursery, and teachers came to our home in Riga. Now we were to go to school with other children. But where would we live? The cottage was not winterized, and our relatives, who were settling near Stockholm, wanted us to come there, but mother felt a pull to the University of Uppsala. She had in her possession her Latvian passport and a record of all her studies at the University of Riga. The University of Riga, at that time, presented every entering student with a leather book that looked rather like a large passport. Each course they studied was described in Latin, and when successfully completed was signed by the professor and stamped with the University Seal. She had three books like that, describing all her studies. Presenting her documents to the university would allow her to enter as a graduate student.

But first she had to find a place to live, a school for us, and she had to earn some money. She heard about an apartment in Uppsala available to refugees and was able to rent one room. To pay for it, she got a job at night while we slept, cleaning coaches of trains. Knowing that other people were sleeping in a room next to ours made that possible. After a few months she was able to find a job at the University translating manuscripts because of her fluency in several languages. Then we moved to our own one-bedroom apartment. The room was furnished with two twin beds that were placed against the wall on either side of the room. One of the twin beds had a trundle pullout bed for me to sleep on. A tall dresser stood at the foot of one of the beds and there was a small table and three chairs by the window. The kitchen was no bigger than a closet. At last, we had privacy and we didn't have to share the bathroom with several other families. We settled in and Mama unpacked the one little suitcase she had brought with us.

Behind the apartment building was a playground for us to explore. Running into our apartment from the playground one afternoon, I discovered mother cutting buttons off my coat. **To my surprise all our cloth-covered buttons were hiding gold coins which Mother tried to hide from me.** Having been discovered she told me not to tell anyone. In the end I saw that she had a little black pouch full of gold coins. I suspect that was the work and provision of Apap and Ama.

At the University of Riga, Mama had studied Law and Economics as well as Library Science. She told me that she wanted to study Law, "so I could carry on an intelligent conversation with Papa." In Uppsala she decided to study meteorology. "Why meteorology"? I asked. "It is totally nonpolitical. Everywhere in the world people need to understand the weather," Mama told me.

That piqued my interest. *If she studies about the clouds and all that is up in the sky, will she learn about Heaven and where God is?* Of course, I did not ask that specifically. I couldn't reveal my secret. But I inquired about everything I could see in the sky. Mama was happy to tell me about the different types of clouds, their names, and that clouds were basically made of water. *So that's not where God is*, I thought to myself. She started to go to church and sent us to Sunday School. On my first day in Sunday School, a sweet teacher was telling us a story from the Bible. She had a felt board on which she put pictures as she spoke. A gray-haired older man depicted God the Father; a brown-haired younger man depicted Jesus the Son of God. I listened attentively, but it all seemed very wordy and left me feeling empty. I was full of questions when I left Sunday School. I even wondered if that teacher knew God. I didn't want to go back to Sunday School — I preferred to go with Mother to the big stone cathedral. There, in that prayed-in place, I felt His presence. There in the holy stillness, even if I wasn't paying full attention to the service, I sensed Him. One Sunday the pastor in the pulpit read a Psalm from the Bible that really piqued my interest. "A father to the fatherless, a defender of widows, is God in his holy dwelling" (Psalm 68:5). That caught my full attention! ***That's why I had that experience on the boat*, I thought to myself, *God is now my father. The pastor said so from the pulpit. He read it from the Bible. Our Heavenly Father is father to the fatherless, I still have a father!***

In the fall, Anna and I started school — I was seven years old. My sister, age nine, seemed to have adjusted well and was flourishing. But not me. I felt awkward. If children or teachers spoke quickly, I could not understand, and I certainly wasn't going to try to speak. When I spoke Swedish, I couldn't say the words the same way the Swedes did. I was so stubborn that a teacher came to our home to talk with my mother, to ascertain if I was able to speak. She wondered if I should go to a special school for children who are mute. Mother was taken aback and said, "At home she talks all the time! Yes, she's able to talk."

The decision was made to have me sit in the front row of the classroom. My very kind teacher, after calling on me for an answer, would come to me and let me whisper my response in his ear. Then he would tell the whole class what I said, and I would nod in agreement, remaining silent. On the playground I would wander around by myself. I did not try to enter any games; I just observed the other children having fun. One day I heard a girl with deformities and disabilities beg some children to join their game. "You couldn't keep up," they said as they ran off. Seeing her disappointment, as she continued to beg them, I felt sorry for her. I spoke up. I said in my broken Swedish, "I will play with you." She looked at me in surprise. "You? Why would I want to play with you?" she said, casting a glance up and down me a disagreeable look on her face. I felt the sting of rejection. Then in my mind I heard the now familiar voice ask, "What are you offering her?" The question came into my mind — pure, nonjudgmental, merely inquiring. *Hmmm. What do I have to offer her*? I thought. *That's a good question. I am isolating myself, meandering around the playground, doing nothing. I am not playing. It's silly to ask her to play with me when I'm not playing.*

I had never been taught to listen to the inward voice of the Holy Spirit. I had never been to Sunday School in Latvia. Ever since He showed Himself to me, however, I had listened for His voice. I decided to step out of my shell and live again. I started to talk and make friends. I stopped being embarrassed about my accent and instead asked my new friends to correct me and help me pronounce the words the right way. The next year I joined a gymnastics team at school and discovered I was quite good at it. I was chosen to represent the school at a citywide demonstration taking place in the large Uppsala stadium. I was beginning to develop some self-confidence.

My mother had developed a friendship at the University with the head of the Department of Meteorology. The family lived in a lovely house on the University campus, and invited us to dinner. Dr. and Mrs. Kuler had a daughter, Karen, who was my age, and we became best friends. Most weekends we found fun adventures riding our bicycles to visit each other.

One Saturday, my mother was dressed in her pretty black skirt with little white flowers. It had pleats sewn down from the waist to the hips, and it showed off her slender waist. At the hips the skirt was free to sway from side to side as she walked. I thought she looked pretty, even though since becoming a widow the only color she wore was black. I asked why she was dressed up. "I'm going out to have lunch with Frau Mueller, my German friend," she said. I was stunned. I stood there with my mouth open, dumbfounded. "How can you say friend and German in the same sentence?" I said with indignation. Mother stopped mid-step, stood still a moment, and then turned around, bending down slightly to look me in the eyes. She said, "My dear child, you need to learn not to paint people with a broad brush. Many, many German people suffered greatly attempting to resist Hitler." Then she gently touched my cheek, turned around and was out the door. *Painting people with a broad brush?* I pondered. I learned that morning that judging people based on what some in a certain country or nationality or ethnic group have done is not right. I realized I had much to learn about forgiving. Now I know that hate corrodes the person who allows it to take root in their mind. That's a hard lesson to learn. My Mother's words, "not to paint people with a broad brush," have stayed with me.

That evening after her luncheon and my outburst, Mama told us about a time in Berlin before the war. In the early 1930s, Papa had work at the University of Berlin, and she had accompanied him on that trip. While he was busy at the university, she enjoyed shopping at the antique stores in the main square. One afternoon people started rushing into the square from every avenue. When so many started to gather, she wondered out loud, why? "Hitler is coming! Hitler is coming!" exclaimed a couple of young, excited ladies. Mama stayed close to the shops, at the back of the crowd that had gathered, and listened as Hitler began shouting his speech. She said that he promised them utopia for free, where everyone would be equally taken care of. He told them that the same aristocrats who got Germany into the costly war were now working in the democratic government, and that they do not understand the hardships of the working man. If only the people would give him all authority and power, he would care for them and life would be fair with equal opportunity. Mama said, "a shiver went down my spine as Hitler spewed promise after promise, with sugarcoated divisive words." "Sugarcoated divisive words? What do you mean?" I asked.

"Hitler used words to divide. He sugarcoated his hateful words about the Jews and aristocrats with promises that he would restore comfortable living standards to the working class which was rightfully theirs. When people became suspicious of each other they blame others for their troubles." "The Nazis did that at home too, didn't they?" I asked, meaning back in Latvia. "Yes, they did. A lot of people became afraid of their Jewish neighbors but actually it was Communist sympathizers who were more guilty of betraying Latvian patriots to the KGB." I was happy when Mama and I could have talks like this. "You told Papa that you heard Hitler speak, didn't you; what did he say?" "When Papa came back from the university that evening, I told him that I had listened to some of Hitler's speech. Papa had already heard about the danger of the Nazis. He had learned from several professors that they feared for the future of Germany." "But why would so many people believe Hitler?" I asked. "Hitler's supporters had infiltrated much of the news media, and people believed what they read in the news. Anyone who criticized Hitler was afraid of being accused of supporting the aristocrats, especially the Kaiser, or being called "Jew lovers" whom the Nazis blamed for the hardship the German people were suffering after the First World War." Mama explained. Then she said, "So girls, you must study always. Always be studying, because as you know, even if you lose everything what you put in your brain no one can take from you, and you will always be able to take care of yourselves. Material things can all be taken from you no one can take what you put it in your brain". I loved having these kinds of conversations with my mother, she never talked down to me and I always had a lot to think about after one of our exchanges. Most of the time she was so busy with work and studying and volunteer work she didn't have time for interaction with Anna and me. We were on our own with "to do lists" she would check off when she got home.

Now that WW2 had ended, we learned that many Latvian people, who feared Stalin's oppressive Communist regime, had fled Latvia. They had followed Germany's retreating army hoping to reach the free world. They were living in refugee camps in western Germany. Mama became involved in sending aid packages to them. She had a job; she was studying for a Master's degree in Meteorology, and she still found time to organize and send aid packages to Latvians living in refugee camps. We were living in a one-bedroom efficiency apartment. Mama had learned to sew. To save money she was learning to replace the heels on our shoes herself. When she told me she was going to be gone all Saturday afternoon to work on aid packages, I felt a little indignant. I thought we could use some aid packages ourselves, especially as Christmas drew near. But she said to me, "You are free to go to school, and I am free to work and study. The people in refugee camps don't have that opportunity. We can help them."

Christmas in a foreign land, without a proper home, and no family — I was not in the mood to celebrate. I think I was just merely surviving, but Mama got a little tree and encouraged us to help her decorate it. We made decorations out of construction paper, and she bought little candles and holders that would snap onto the branches and a pretty star for the top. On Christmas Eve, Mama had accepted an invitation to have dinner with a refugee family in our neighborhood. When we arrived at their apartment, I overheard Anna talking to their children, who were older than I. "Katrina is young, she believes in Santa Claus. So be careful what you say." *Young enough to believe in Santa Claus?* I did believe in Santa Claus. *What's wrong with that?* At home in Riga, we had to memorize a poem to recite to Santa if he should arrive before we went to bed. That was our Christmas preparation. *What did they mean*? The boy around my sister's age asked me with a smirk on his face, "Do you believe in Santa Claus?" He said it in such a sarcastic way, I gathered there was something wrong and childish about believing in Santa Claus. I didn't answer. I turned my back to him, drew Mama aside, and questioned her. I was feeling very angry and certainly didn't want to cry. I was seven years old and didn't want to be called a baby. Mama quietly explained that it was a story based on a kind bishop who lived long ago, who loved young people, especially children, and brought them presents when they were going to be without a present to celebrate the birthday of Jesus. Tears stung my eyes. I didn't want them to run down my cheeks. I gritted my teeth in anger. I did not like to be fooled. *Why was it fun for adults to fool children and then laugh about it behind their backs?* I thought. I felt very hurt. I was glad to leave after dinner and go to church.

The candlelit sanctuary of the ancient cathedral was decorated with flowers and evergreens. It was awe-inspiring! In that beautiful, grand space I felt that this was a real celebration. This was not a fairy tale; this was real and true. Then we sang *"Oh come all ye children with peace in your mind, to Bethlehem's stable"* and many other familiar Christmas carols. The same carols that we had sung in Latvian we sang in Swedish. After the lovely service we walked home through a snow-covered landscape. In the stillness, on that cold late night, the snow squeaked under our feet, stars twinkled in the sapphire sky, and an illumined star hung in every window we passed. The three of us were going to be alright after all, I thought. It was a beautiful night. At home we lit the candles on our little tree and sang a Christmas carol or two. Then Mama gave each of us a present. I was so happy she had bought herself one too. I don't remember mine, but hers was a little silver cup. We drank some hot cocoa while watching the candlelight flickering on the branches of the tree. I went to bed happy after celebrating Jesus's birthday.

One night I was awakened from my sleep by Mama's voice sounding like a frog's croak, "Anna, wake up!" "What's wrong?" we said in unison as my sister turned on the light. "Get help," Mama said between gasps for air as her face contorted from pain. Panic rose like bile in my throat. I followed Anna out the door as she ran to get help. We knocked as hard as we could on the door of the neighboring apartment. We knocked and kept knocking until finally somebody heard us. At last, a sleepy voice asked, without opening the door, what the commotion was. After explaining about Mama, they opened the door and invited us in and then went to help Mama.

What would happen to Anna and me if she died? I thought. As long as she was near, she was my stability in this unstable world, but what if we became orphans? What happens to orphans? I would not want to be separated from my big sister. I had heard some dreadful stories about orphanages. As Anna and I huddled together, in the hallway of these kind strangers' apartment, I sunk into a swamp of fear. Deeper and deeper, it pulled me with every tragic image that came to mind. Fear seemed to close my ears and squeeze my breath. Filled with dread, there was no room for the voice of my heavenly Father. I didn't seek him. I descended into the hell of fear. I learned that night how destructive and debilitating fear can be. Fear can pull you down into blinding depths of despair. God only intends fear to warn us of danger, not to drag us into despair. That painful lesson would help me many times in the years to come.

Our neighbors arranged for an ambulance to take Mama to the hospital. We learned that she needed surgery, therefore, it was arranged that I should take the train to Stockholm and live with my Aunt Janina and Uncle Jānis Terins, in Norcherping for the rest of the summer. I didn't want to go, but soon realized my protests were adding stress to the situation. I was nine years-old and felt very grownup when I boarded the train by myself. Bishop Terins was my Godfather and Janina, his wife, was my Papa's oldest sister. They met my train in Stockholm, I would be living with them for about a month, I was told. They had two teenage sons, one already heading to university. Their apartment was much larger than ours, and my aunt didn't go to work during the day. It was nice to have her company. Their sons, my cousins, worked in an ice cream factory during the summer while school was out. My favorite part of the day was when they came home from work, because every evening they brought home a different flavor of ice cream. I could have as much as I wanted, since the boys themselves had gotten tired of eating so much ice cream.

On weekends, Aunt Janina and I would walk to visit the families of my other aunts and uncles who lived nearby. We made the rounds from apartment to apartment. Aunt Daila and Uncle Paul's children were close to my age. Our Grandmother, Papa's Mother, Oma lived with them. Their home was crowded, relaxed, and fun. I didn't have to worry about behaving like a little grown-up. The

Tepfer's home was not in the same neighborhood but Aunt Janina and I made our way to visit them as well. I was very fond of their three daughters; it was great fun to reconnect with my cousins.

On weekdays I spent a lot of time in my bedroom, reading and daydreaming about when my mother was healthy, my Papa was alive, and we had a real home. In my mind I relived those happy times. I pictured our summer cottage, Mama playing the piano, and Papa singing and teaching me to dance the waltz. Daydreaming about the past I hummed a tune and danced around the room by myself. Recollections of home warmed my heart, during moments of loneliness. Some evenings, my Uncle would come into the little bedroom, which probably had been one of their boy's rooms. While I stayed with them, they shared another small room. Uncle Terins would pray with me before turning the light out. Although the Terins home back in Jurmala, Latvia, was across the lane from our summer cottage, and Uncle Terins was my Godfather, I had not known an intimate relationship with him. He had been a busy Pastor of Dome Cathedral in Riga, and their children were already in their teens. During those brief prayer times, however, I felt such loving intimacy. Without talking about it, I felt we shared the same secret, that Heaven was real and God IS. In the fourteenth chapter of First Corinthians, the twenty-fifth verse, we read "God is truly here among us," even though we can't understand how.

When I returned home to Uppsala, it seemed my sister was a lot older than she was when I left a month earlier. Mama seemed more delicate as she greeted me with loving hugs. My sister seemed a lot bossier too. Every morning she walked Mama to work and carried her briefcase for her. In the evening she went to meet her and to carry her briefcase home. I wanted to help do that but was told by Anna to "stay home and tidy up." I didn't take well to being bossed around by my sister, and I thought walking with Mama was a lot more fun than housework. Mama would write letters to her parents in Latvia, and when she received a reply, she would read them to us. "Apap and Ama want us to come home to Latvia," I said with glee after listening to Mama read a letter. *The Soviets were restoring order and the war was over*, the letter said. Mama looked so sad as she explained to us that her parents were probably pressured to write that letter. "Notice the final paragraph talked about a farm they had visited. They wrote about the chickens, and that it was better for chickens to stay where they were for the sake of their health," Mama added, "I think the chicken represented you and Anna. I think they were trying to tell us we are safer where we are."

Communists have long-term goals and long memories — they don't forget to punish anyone opposed to their goal of world domination. After some years, we started receiving letters from the Communist sympathizers who now worked in the Latvian Embassy in Stockholm. Any letters Mama would not share with us we read while she was at work. "If you do not accept our kind offer of free transport home to Latvia, when the Soviet Union occupies Sweden, it will not be so comfortable for you," was written in one letter. I recalled the stories of my young cousin's arrest by soldiers at night. They had been locked in a cattle car for a long time, shipped to Siberia without adequate food or clothing for the bitter cold and long winters. They were prisoners and slaves, having to work for the Soviet war machine. Some men from the embassy came to talk with Mama. They were Latvian Communists and Russians who had been sent to the Latvian Embassy by the Soviets who now occupied Latvia. In the early twentieth century Marx's writings became popular with some people all over Europe as kingdoms were falling. His writings were taught and lauded in some distinguished universities in America as well. Marxism even influenced a few people in the Roosevelt administration, who expressed an interest in studying "this new economic thought" and wanted to observe how it was going to be implemented in the Soviet Union. In Latvia also there were idealists, avowed atheists, who supported the Communist uprising in Russia with hope that they would establish this new economic idea, and it would be better for the working class.

When they came to our apartment to talk with Mama, I could see that their visit upset her. *Why were they picking on our Mama?* I wondered. As far as I knew they were not harassing our relatives who lived near Stockholm. Was it because she was a vulnerable widow? Now, looking back I realize it was probably because my father had communicated with Prime Minister Churchill's and President Roosevelt's Governments through the Latvian embassy in Sweden. The United States considered Stalin an Ally in the war against Hitler. The US armed the Russian military afterwards and helped them to become a powerful force. All intelligence reports were available to Russia as an ally, during the Second World War. My Father had informed his American and British contacts that after the underground sent them information, Russian forces had attacked the position of our underground patriots. He tried to warn the United States and England of the danger of trusting the Soviet Russians and he informed them of the brutality of their occupation of the Baltic countries.

The United States informed Papa that the Soviets, as part of the Alliance, should not be spied upon, and that he was not to send information about the Communist regime, since they were only interested in any information he could provide about the Nazis. The Soviet Union would have seen all the communiqués from my father, with their ambitions to occupy the Baltic territories, and they would have wanted the Latvian underground resistance destroyed. With their ambition of world domination, I wondered if they had their spies leak information to the Nazis about Papa's work? Was that how Hitler found out that my father was the head of the Latvian underground government? Did Communist spies make his identity known to the Nazi SS, even though Papa had used a pseudonym? Is that why Hitler charged Papa with espionage?

The saying "The enemy of my enemy is my friend" might have been the thinking of the United States at the time, but that does not make for a true alliance. The US armed the Soviet Union in World War 2, and later, in what was called "the cold war," reaped the bitter consequences of having done so. As a ten-year-old I did not know all that. I didn't know 15,424 Latvian citizens were deported in 1941, alongside my Aunt, and that approximately 70% of them perished. I didn't know that if Mama had yielded to their request for us to return to Latvia in 1948, we might have been among the 42,125 deported to slave labor camps in Siberia in March of 1949. Knowing what had happened to my aunt and cousins at the hands of Communists was enough. I was very much afraid of those people who came from the Latvian Embassy, which now was under Soviet control.

One day, the Latvian Communists arrived when Mama was not home. They asked to come in and speak with Anna and me. Through the closed door we told them we were not allowed to let people in when Mama was not home. They continued to knock and talk to us through the door. We became so frightened we pushed a dresser, which was taller than I, against the front door and looked around to see what else we could use to reinforce our barricade. Not long after the knocking stopped Mama was at the door and couldn't get in. She could not persuade us to let her in. We told her to go outside — we wanted to see that she was alone. She had no choice. She went downstairs and out the front door of the apartment building and looked up at us. She said, "See, I am alone!" Looking out the second story window we could see no strangers, but I was still not satisfied. Threatening men could be standing in the doorway under the overhang where I couldn't see them. "Go out to the street and walk up and down," I said. I thought *that once she was out in the street, she would be far enough away from anyone threatening her, and she would be able to run for help.* She knew we weren't going to let her in until she complied, so she walked up and down the street again telling me, "Girls, there is no one here but me!" Anna was already dissembling our barricade by the time I said, "Okay, I see it is safe." Later in the evening, after we told Mama what they said, we all laughed about it. My fear was replaced with a feeling of satisfaction. I felt empowered! We were not helpless children; Anna and I had defended our family! Mama told us about her plans to emigrate to America. She explained that a few years earlier she had gone to the US Embassy to apply for a visa. It might take a few more years, she explained. She instructed us not to talk about that possibility outside our family.

A friend of my Mother's, who was an artist, had emigrated to South Africa. Her letters were fascinating. She told us about her South African friends and that, because of apartheid, she had moved out of the city to avoid getting into trouble with the police. Europeans were not allowed to socialize with the native people, which I thought was incomprehensible. She was building a ceramic factory with the help of South African workers, whom she had come to love. Out in the Bush it was safe for them to be friends, interact and dine together. She said they were quickly learning about her technique of baking clay into useful and artistic objects. She also sent us lovely photographs. My sister and I wanted to go to Africa so we could have a friend with skin the color of dark chocolate! Chocolate was my favorite treat and, long before it was considered racist, *Little Black Sambo* became my favorite book. I thought Sambo was so clever, he outsmarted the lion, the king of the jungle. He was as brave as I wanted to be. However, Mother said that in America we would be guaranteed freedom. In America we would not have to worry about apartheid police, and we would not have to fear any government authorities because the government answers to the people. Their founding Constitution guarantees that, she told us.

The botanical garden in Uppsala had several ponds with water lilies of many different varieties and colors. Anna and I liked to ride our bikes to the park in the summertime and play hide and go-seek and other games around the ponds while Mama was at work. One day a couple stopped us while we skipped from rock to rock. Anna had studied English for a year and understood that they wanted to take our picture with the waterlilies. They told us that they were from America and invited us to come for a visit. Anna told them that we wanted to go to Africa so we could have a friend with chocolate color skin. They laughed and said we could have that in America as well and showed us pictures. I decided I wanted to go to America as Mama had planned, but my sister still tried to persuade Mama to move to Africa.

When winter approached, we looked forward to snow — the more the better. If the streets were snow packed, we could ski to school. At school, everyone just stuck the skis into a deep snowbank and went to class. At other times we took a sled to school. In early December, my friends and I decided to surprise our teacher. This was the dear man who allowed me to whisper my answers into his ear when I started school in Sweden. On the thirteenth of December, which was the shortest day of the year in the old Julian Calendar, the Swedes celebrated St. Lucia in remembrance of the loving young girl, Lucia, one of the earliest martyrs. She was killed by the Romans in 304 A.D. because she would not renounce her faith in Jesus. The story goes that she brought sweet breads and the light of Christ to people, especially children, living in darkness. My friends and I contacted our teacher's wife, who agreed to leave a key to their front door under the mat for us. Very early in the morning on the thirteenth of December, while it was still dark, we planned to go into their apartment to wake him up and serve him coffee and pastries while singing the Santa Lucia song in the candlelit bedroom. I was so excited, my mother helped me put on my white gown and my red sash over my winter jumper and a sparkling gold garland around my head. Then off I went to meet my friends. The five of us had already decided who would be Lucia — the girl with the lightest blonde hair. She got to wear the crown of evergreen with several candles circling her head and carry the tray with coffee and pastry. The rest of us, her court, carried a candle. Once we were outside our teacher's door, we lit all the candles in Lucia's crown of evergreens and the one each of us carried, and processed into their apartment and down the hall to their bedroom singing the Lucia song. What joy it was to see our teacher's surprise as we entered the dark room, the light from our candles casting a warm glow that revealed his smile as his eyes blinked open. With sleepy eyes and a broad smile, he thanked us. We served them both coffee and pastries in bed and then departed. After leaving his home we visited whomever we thought needed to be cheered up. When the sun rose on a new day we headed home. In the dim light of an early sunrise, we saw other groups of friends, in white gowns, carrying trays of goodies and a thermos of coffee. Some college students were riding bicycles through the snow wearing white sheets with a whole cut in the center for the head. Their Lucia had a white mop for hair on his head, and the crown of evergreen held it in place. He was balancing a tray in his right hand as he bicycled down the street with his friends. We laughed as they rode past us singing lustily!

As winter wore on my health suffered. I had sinus infections, and ear infections, and I caught every contagious infection going around. Finally, our last year in Sweden, I landed in the hospital with what was diagnosed as rheumatic fever. Lying alone in a long ward, with empty beds along both sides of the room, all I had to look at were starched white sheets and blankets on all the empty beds. I had nothing to do, so I was bored stiff. I was told to rest. Every day when the cleaning lady came in, I tried to engage her in conversation. She wore a starched white apron and was very efficient and thorough, but not interested in talking with me. After every corner and every surface had been carefully cleaned and rinsed, I saw her leaning over at the door with a Q-tip cleaning the keyhole. I thought that was funny and said with a laugh, "How could dirt get in the keyhole?" Without stopping what she was doing she said in her sing song Swedish, "Jah-h don't you think dust and germs can get inside a keyhole?" Despite the isolation in a sterile hospital ward, once I was finally released and returned home, I came down with the mumps. During our last winter in Uppsala, Sweden, I spent many months in bed.

My mother had met Dag Hammarskjold, who was familiar with my father's work on International Law and Economics. Dr. Hammarskjold was a Swedish economist and diplomat. A few years after their meeting, in 1953 to be exact, just as he was appointed Secretary-General of the United Nations (an office he held until his death in a plane crash in 1961, while on a mission for the UN to the Congo), Mama developed a friendship with him and his two spinster sisters. The three Hammarskjold's lived together, and the sisters doted on their brother. The sisters said, "His mind is on academic and world matters. Practical things, like wearing his galoshes on a rainy day, would never cross his mind if we didn't remind him." We always enjoyed having Tea in their lovely sitting room. When they heard that I was sick and had to stay at home in bed all alone, they brought me a beautiful doll that had belonged to their mother. Her face, arms, and legs were made of porcelain. She had exquisite, delicate features and lovely natural hair. She was a wonderful companion. I would sit her beside me on the bed and take cork stoppers out of all the medicine bottles, place them in a semicircle in front of her, and pretend that they were her teeth and I was a dentist. I drilled holes in the corks with a knitting needle and filled them with the foil I saved from candy wrappers. Soon all the medicine bottles had unique, foil-dotted cork stoppers. I think I liked dentists because in Riga our dentist was a lady-friend of Mama's, who always complimented me on my good teeth and gave me rides up and down in the dental chair. I wanted to be a dentist when I grew up. My sister brought homework from school so I wouldn't miss half a year of school. With schoolwork, make-believe games, and morning and afternoon naps, the days passed by quickly. The doctor came to our home to examine me every so often.

When spring arrived, I was finally allowed to get up and go outside. I was so excited to be able to be outside and go to the playground and see some children. The playground was behind our apartment house. I followed my friends to the back of our apartment complex where, after playing a while, I fainted. The next thing I knew I was being carried up the stairs to our apartment in the strong arms of a man. We had lived in that apartment for five years; and he knew which apartment was my home. Mama, who was in the basement laundry room, had seen me on the ground and hurried upstairs. She called the doctor, who came to us before the end of the day. After he examined me, and listened to my heart, he and Mama went out into the hall, I heard him quietly talking with Mama in the hallway. She asked him if a sea voyage or a trip to Switzerland would be good for me? "Yes, I think it might be very good, but I would be concerned about the voyage. Traveling there might be too strenuous for her." I didn't know at the time that Mama, having discovered that our Visa application had vanished from the file at the US Embassy, had joined with friends and bought a large sailboat as an investment and transportation to the US.

The month of June was full of activity. Anytime Mama was home from work she was busy packing and purging. It's not that we had accumulated so many things that needed to be discarded, but we could only take bare necessities, which was a lot more than the one small suitcase and two backpacks we had when we arrived in Sweden. Anna was sent on many errands and given lists of chores to accomplish while Mama was at work. I was told to rest. When the day came to board the train, I was not allowed to carry anything. We were only bringing one small suitcase, two very large suitcases, and some handbags. Mama would not let me do anything to be helpful. She kept saying, "Anna pick that up. Katrina sit down. Anna carry that." My poor sister. Every time I tried to get up to help, I was scolded. I was instructed just to sit and not touch my face, even if my nose was itching. Mama would say, "Exercise self-control. Do you want to rub the germs from other people's hands onto your face?"

As the electric train glided through the Swedish countryside, passing villages, forests, and pastures, I took in the scenes rushing by. I was excited about our adventure. We were in a comfortable train, and we did not have to fear soldiers or hide in barns under the hay. I was not going to miss our one room apartment, which never felt like home - only like temporary shelter. The city of Uppsala was beautiful, and I had made dear friends there whom

I would miss, but it had never felt like home. If home is defined as your cozy, secure place, then only Mama was home to me now. I was excited to be traveling with her and Anna, the three of us together without fear or apprehension.

Our destination was Gothenburg, a port city on the southwestern coast of Sweden. It's a long way from Uppsala, which is located north of Stockholm. In Gothenburg our sailboat would be waiting for us. Mama told us it was a large sailboat — much larger than the boat we came to Sweden on. She said it had sailed from Canada across the Atlantic before they purchased it. The plan was to cross the Atlantic Ocean in the month of July, when the sea is more likely to be calm.

Upon arriving in Gothenburg and making our way to the port where our beautiful sailboat was docked, we learned some bad news. Our captain had been in the Latvian Merchant Marines and had been captain of ships that sailed around the horn of Africa, where ships can encounter very rough seas. He felt confident in his ability to sail to America, although it would be his first time to cross the Atlantic. He had inspected this ship carefully and discovered that one of the three masts appeared to have stress damage. He had ordered a new mast, and we would need to delay our departure. He also informed Mama that he did not want to depart until he had spare parts for every eventuality. Mama seemed a little concerned, but I didn't mind. She was not working, and we could spend all day together. We moved into our small windowless berth below deck. Along one wall we had a triple bunkbed. I wanted the top bunk; it was so close to the overhead that my sister didn't mind. I was short for my age, just short enough to be able to sit up in bed without hitting my head. My twelfth birthday was coming up soon. Outside our berth was a large room with a long table in the center and benches attached to the floor. The table had a raised edge to prevent dishes from sliding off when the boat rocked at sea. There were doors on both sides of that main room. The captain had assigned berths according to family size. All six families had invested in this boat. I thought it was rather nice to have this time to familiarize myself with the boat while it was docked and explore every nook and cranny.

After we had settled in, Mama took us on tours of the city in the mornings. My favorite part of the day was when she allowed us to go to the beach. All the children were running in and out of the water, having a wonderful time. She tried to keep me sitting beside her, but I couldn't stay still for long. In Uppsala we went swimming in lakes or rivers. As far as I was concerned, the beach far surpassed any other form of summer entertainment. Soon I was running in and out of the water with the other children, despite Mother's concerned protests. I seemed to get stronger with each day.

Chapter Nine: *SAILING ACROSS THE ATLANTIC*

"Eternal Father, strong to save, whose arm hath bound the restless wave, Who bidd'st the mighty ocean deep its own appointed limits keep: O hear us when we cry to thee for those in peril on the sea." by William Whiting

Movement of the boat awakened me early one morning. I climbed down from my bunk in the dark and went up to the deck. Far to the east, the sun's rays were reaching for the horizon with a light golden glow in the gray sky. I thought, *back there, far away, is my home in Latvia, and we are sailing farther and farther away.* I felt a little melancholy for the first time. I remembered then that if I were in Latvia, strangers would be assigned to share our apartment and our summer cottage would not be ours and Papa would not be there. I thought about my cousins in Stockholm. When would I see them again? I turned around and looked to the west and wondered what awaited us behind that black curtain of night sky the sun had not yet reached. I felt a gentle sea breeze on my face and thought to myself, *We are sailing to a safe new life, far away from those Communists who harassed us*, and joy dawned with the new day. "Katrina, it's too early for you to be up," Mother said to me. "Go back to sleep."

The next time I emerged from our cabin, the sun was shining through a thin layer of clouds, and the sails were full of wind. We were crossing the North Sea at a fine clip, our keel cutting through the blue and gray waves, raising sprays of white foam. I began to feel a little queasy from the rocking. There was nothing but water on the horizon, nothing else to fasten my eyes to.

"Ah! Katrina is going to feed the fishes," Mr. Zveinieks laughed and came over to help me. He lifted me up and held me as I leaned over the railing so I could empty my stomach. I was leaning over the side as far as I dared and greatly appreciated Mr. Zveinieks holding onto me. I didn't want to soil our boat nor did I want to fall overboard. I was not the only one with seasickness that first day at sea. Captain John said we would get our sea legs soon and feel better. I went forward to the bow. With more wind in my face, I was relieved that I felt a little better. If I was going to feel so nauseous this whole trip it was not going to be the fun adventure I anticipated. After several hours, we altered our direction from west to southwest and south. Off in the distance land was visible. That was exciting, I thought, and asked what I was looking at. I was told it was Scotland. I stared at the rocky cliffs along the shore as we passed by, and getting my mind off my seasickness, I realized I was feeling better. I had no idea that far in the future Scotland would come to mean a great deal to me. We passed through the English Channel at night with a storm beating our boat. As I lay in my bunk I thought, *I will never get my sea legs. I have never been this sick in my life.* I had emptied my stomach and now was vomiting green bile. Mama gave me a damp towel to wipe my mouth. I laid my head back on my pillow and recalled our Baltic Sea crossing. We had encountered nothing this severe. I remembered then that we were not alone — my Heavenly Father saw me and was with me on the Baltic Sea, and He is with us now. A peace filled my heart with assurance, and I heard in my mind. *All will be well.* I whispered back, "Yes! All will be well!" Then I fell asleep.

After passing south of England we turned west-southwest. The sea was calm with gently rolling waves, and the sky was a clear blue. The wind in my face was warm. Everyone enjoyed sailing in what we called the tropical Atlantic. We had most of our evening meals up on the deck. After dinner, some of the men brought out musical instruments to accompany us as we sang Latvian folk songs. Latvians have an ancient culture and have archived thousands of folk songs. Because traditionally every party includes singing, most people know most of those songs by heart. This comforting, peaceful mood, with familiar music and the swooshing splash of waves as the wind drove our boat westward, evolved into excitement when someone shouted, "Look! I see land!" Off in the distance, the Azores Islands rose out of the water. We knew that the next day we would dock and walk on solid ground once more. The Azores are an autonomous region of Portugal, comprised of nine islands, volcanic in origin. They lie just east of the mid-Atlantic ridge. During World War 2 German U-boats had refueled there as they patrolled the Atlantic Ocean and attacked ships crossing to Europe. In 1943, on October the third a German U-boat managed to get inside the convoy escorting USAT Dorchester transporting 904 troops to Europe, and launched torpedoes sinking the Dorchester. Only 230 men were saved. That U boat had probably refueled at the Azores.

Britain negotiated a contract with Portugal to establish a Navy base on one of the islands. Thereafter the U-boats could no longer refuel in the Azores and the US and British Navy tracked U-boats from that port and our ships were less vulnerable as they crossed the Atlantic.

The tropical beauty of the Azores was a delight and feast for the eyes. Trees and flowers, I had never seen before, emitted unusual and delightful fragrances that engaged my senses. As we stepped off the boat onto stable ground, I could still feel the rocking of the boat beneath my feet. The town rose from the port up the side of a dormant volcanic mountain. The road wound its way up the mountain. In the village we entered a cafe for lunch. Sitting at an outdoor table we could see our sailboat at the port far down below. From where we sat the captain and crew looked not much bigger than ants scurrying around. At an outdoor market we were thrilled at the great variety of delicious fruit. We stocked up on watermelons, pineapples, bananas, and oranges — fruit that would last on board. I had never tasted watermelon before and enjoyed its sweet juice. It became my favorite. The people were so nice and welcoming and told us that they hadn't had many civilian visitors since before the Second World War.

Once we set sail again, the grownups persuaded Captain John to sail due west instead of following the ship lanes across the Atlantic as he had planned. Why not sail towards Florida and then up the coast, they suggested. We could continue to enjoy the warm climate and calm seas. I was all for that and excited when the captain relented and started studying his maps. Day after day we enjoyed warm days, eating meals up on the deck and singing folk songs in the evening. We played board games and card games. I enjoyed having Mama leisurely playing games with us. Anna learned how to play chess from the older boys. I wanted to stay close to Mama. For the five years we lived in Sweden she had worked nonstop — now she was available to me emotionally and physically. As my health rebounded, I could tell she no longer seemed concerned whether I rested or not.

One evening the captain and crew seemed to be struggling with the sails. There was no wind to fill the sails; the air and sea were unusually calm. The captain started the motor. No one seemed concerned, and we thought that most likely the wind would pick up in the morning. The rhythmic chugging of the motor sounded like background drums for our evening songs. The next evening, as we were singing a lovely old, slow ballad, "*Put Vejins*," accompanied by accordion, guitar, and harmonica, the background beat of the engine caught and stopped. The accordion music stopped, then the harmonica, and guitar, and the voices of the singers trailed off one by one. Most of us sat still in the eerie silence. There was no sound of wind or waves or motion. The captain and crew rushed about to ascertain why the engine had shut down. We had left the shipping lanes and had not seen another vessel for several days. The adults seemed concerned. I was enjoying the stillness - we had been in constant motion for weeks. I looked about at the beautiful blue-green, clear sparkling water, to the southwest of our position I noticed what appeared to be a landmass. I wondered, *is it an island that was flat and unexpected?* Our Captain checked his maps - there were no islands, no markings, but he did note seaweed. In the middle of the Atlantic, where the North Atlantic current moves east and the South Atlantic currents move west, what appears to look like an island to the eye is called the Saragossa Sea, a floating "island" of seaweed that is unnavigable. The blades of our motor had been wrapped in seaweed. Ships do not venture near the Saragossa Sea.

Our desire to enjoy the warm weather had caused us unwittingly to sail too close. A couple of the young crew members had to take turns diving down to examine the rudder blades. They informed us that cords of seaweed were wound tightly around the blades; they were unyielding and impossible to pull apart with bare hands. The captain had the crew working tirelessly, diving down time after time with knives and sheers, holding their breath, cutting the ropes of seaweed to free the blades. While they were working hard, some of the men in our group had the brilliant idea to go swimming. The captain accommodated them by casting out a large net. I wondered if it was to protect the swimmers from sharks or from being pulled under? My sister appeared on deck in her bathing suit and wanted to jump in. Mother shrieked in protest that a big fish would bite her. Mr. Zveinieks, who was already enjoying the warm, clear water, reassured her that he hadn't seen any sharks.

“Nu, I don’t know; do you really think it’s safe?” Mama said with concern in her voice. That's all Anna needed to hear. Without hesitation she jumped off the side, about a sixteen-foot drop, I guessed, to the water below. We watched her descend a long way down in the clear blue water, and then she swam back up to the surface. I watched in amazement and admiration and kept peering into the water wherever she swam, to be sure I could warn her if a fish approached. She was so happy to go swimming in the middle of the Atlantic Ocean. I wished that I could have joined her, but I was not a strong swimmer, and I knew Mama would never allow it.

The crew worked for hours, diving down time after time, cutting away the unyielding strands of seaweed. We didn’t have scuba equipment on board — they could only work at cutting the seaweed as long as they could hold their breath. After several hours of strenuous work, we once more heard the *chug, chug* of our repaired motor. Loud cheers and applause embraced the tired crew. The captain turned the bow north/north-west and was not going to be persuaded to sail into anymore adventures.

The next day our sails filled with wind again and within a day or so we noticed other ships passing in the distance to starboard. We were safely on course. Our vessel was not equipped with a radio or radar. Our Captain knew how to navigate by the stars with a sextant — he assessed our progress each evening and morning to keep us on course. For days on end there was not much to see except water, waves, the everchanging cloud formations, and occasional flying fish or a pod of dolphins.

As we neared the American coast, a thick fog enveloped us. Captain John sounded the foghorn rhythmically, but I noticed that, as we sailed farther east, the lonesome call of the foghorn was all around us in the distance. It sounded like lonely ships calling to each other in thick fog. Always curious, I walked over to the captain on the bridge to ask if we were close to land with the toot of foghorns coming closer and closer. I found him too busy to interrupt with my questions. “I have gone over my calculations,” I overheard him saying as he studied his maps. “I am convinced our position is correct. We are at least one hundred nautical miles from the coast. So why are there so many ships out here in one location?” Just then the lookout, whom the captain had posted upfront, shouted anxiously that a ship was coming right at us from starboard. I ran forward to see as the captain made a very sharp turn towards port. The foghorn sounded the piercing alarm of a ship in danger at sea. The oncoming vessel did not change course but continued coming straight toward us through the fog. Anna had been distracted from her chess game by the sudden and drastic turn of our sailboat and emerged from below, just as we were hit broadside. Both of us tumbled to the deck. I heard her whisper, "The Russians have caught us." Stunned, we got back on our feet and looked up at a large commercial vessel.

The men who peered down at us over the side of the derelict ship spoke English. That was a relief — the Russians had not caught us, but now what? We had a large hole in the side of our beautiful wooden sailboat. How had this happened? Their ship was navigating by radar only, which doesn't recognize a wooden boat. I wondered if their lookout had gone below for a moment. Was there no one on deck to hear our foghorn and warn their captain? When Captain John tried to communicate with the American sailors, we realized we had a language barrier. None of us spoke English fluently. However, we understood their inquiry. They asked why we had not sounded our foghorn, to which every voice on our deck, including mine, responded, "Yes we did, constantly!"

This was not a time for recrimination, however — we had to mend our vessel and make it seaworthy. They shot ropes down to us, and our crew tied them off so that crewmen from their ship could rappel down to us. They brought ice cream and other treats with them, which were set aside for later. As much as I was looking forward to ice cream, I was more interested to see how they would help us repair the hole in the side of our boat. Wood was harvested from the interior of our boat wherever possible. Two men wearing a harness were lowered down the side to where the hole was. They seemed to be stuffing it with odds and ends, I thought as I watched, leaning over the side as far as I dared. Then they hammered the harvested wood across the hole. It was not very attractive, but they deemed it waterproof.

The American seamen who had come onboard explained to us that the reason all these ships were circling far from shore was because a hurricane was coming up the east coast. Mama immediately got out her dictionary to ascertain the meaning of the word "*hurricane*." "Ah, a bad storm," Mama said. *"Ve have sailed through bad storms already, it vill be all right."* The Latvian alphabet does not have a W; it took us a long time to learn to pronounce a W instead of saying V. The seamen chuckled at her nonchalance and said, "A hurricane is more than a bad storm. It's a very, very big, and very, very bad storm."

The Coast Guard had been summoned to our aid. After much debate and some consternation, it was decided that we should try to make for shore because the storm seemed to turn east a little, and the brunt of the storm could reach our position. With the wind swirling, we lowered the sails and tied them down. Accompanied by the Coast Guard cutter we motored toward Boston.

Very soon we learned the meaning of the word *hurricane*. I lay in my top bunk holding on to the guardrail. I had already emptied my stomach in my pail, including the delicious ice cream I had consumed. Now there was nothing to do but hold on tightly to the guardrail, as our sailboat seemed to climb a steep mountain and then fall over the edge, landing with such force that I felt everything vibrate. My body was lifted up off the mattress more than once. **The story of Jesus walking on water to the disciples, who were in a sailboat in the middle of a storm, came into my mind.** I was not afraid, amazingly, I don't recall feeling any fear except that of falling out of my bunk. I didn't want to be thrown out of bed and land on the floor by my mother's lower bunk; that would upset her a great deal. Oh, certainly I realized that we might die if Jesus did not calm the storm for us as He had done for his frightened disciples. I talked to Him and told Him that I knew He could see us in our current predicament. If we were to die, I looked forward to seeing Him. I asked Him to please comfort my mother so that she would not be afraid.

I had never told her about the experience I had when we crossed the Baltic Sea. I thought that she might not know how wonderful Heaven is. I knew she talked to God because I had seen her in deep prayer many times, and Anna had read the Bible from cover to cover, but I wondered if they knew the wonders we have to look forward to? "Jesus," I whispered something to this affect; "Jesus, if we come to you tonight, the three of us would come together, and they will see what I saw and know your all-knowing, all enveloping love."

Our sailboat rocked and rolled and dropped from high waves time after time. Other times tall waves came crashing down on top of our boat with great force. I could feel our boat shiver and hear the motor of the sump pump working nonstop. Eventually the sump pump could not keep up with the amount of water falling on top of our boat. I heard voices outside our berth and some of the men joined the crew, who had tied themselves to the masts. They formed a bucket brigade, trying to keep up with all the water that was crashing down on us. Hour after hour they worked as the boat pitched and bucked, and rolled, and water slushed on the floor of our berth. I don't think a roller coaster ride has ever been created anywhere on earth that can be compared to the ride we had at sea in that hurricane. Forty-foot waves crashed down over our vessel, the Coast Guard crew later told us. At times they thought we had gone down. But back up to the surface we popped, like a cork out of the water, thanks be to God, who was looking out for us and the brave men who formed the bucket brigade. Our lovely, old, scarred sailboat survived the worst the ocean could throw at her and brought us safely to shore in America with help from my Father above.

As soon as we entered the calmer waters of Boston Harbor, I dashed up to the deck, ever curious to see this new land we were approaching, the land that was to be my safe home. I was mesmerized, searching the horizon. Mother came to fetch me — she wanted to make sure I looked presentable when we stepped ashore. That was not an easy task after what we had endured. Exercising all the patience and self-restraint I could muster, obediently I went down below, washed up, changed my clothes, and combed my hair. Mama had already cleaned up the mess in our cabin, and she was busy packing. My excitement could hardly be contained. *What was awaiting us?* I wondered.

After we docked, immigration officials came on board to speak with our Captain and escort us to an immigration office. Mama presented her Latvian passport and asked for asylum. She had papers from Stutthof Concentration Camp and stated that Papa was charged with the crime of ESPIONAGE. He had been arrested because, as the head of the Underground Government resistance in Latvia, he had communicated with the Allies during the World War II. An immigration official looked up and said, "The war is over.

Why couldn't you return to Latvia?" Mama was prepared with her answer. "My husband and I worked clandestinely to resist the Soviet occupation of Latvia in 1940. It would be very dangerous for me and my daughters to return now. I am sure you know the Soviet Army occupies our country, and they want to integrate it into the Soviet Union. We are stateless at the present," she calmly explained. I remember the sound of his fingers clicking the keys of the typewriter, recording a summation of her words.

The Boston Globe newspaper had heard about a sailboat, which had been damaged at sea, carrying several families of immigrants, but had survived sailing through the hurricane. They sent a reporter to interview us. Everyone seemed amazed at our survival. I felt embraced by the warm welcome of all these strangers in Boston. Even the Coast Guard and immigration officials — everyone seemed to celebrate our survival.

The legal situation was not quite so simple. Mama was allowed to telephone the contact person for the church in Tennessee that had agreed to sponsor us, a Mrs. Keese. The immigration officials spoke with her and explained that we would be transferred to Ellis Island since we didn't have a legal Visa. The immigration staff in Boston was so kind and empathetic. When it was time for us to depart, they came out to say goodbye as if they were old friends. With a heart full of joy, I didn't notice when I boarded the bus that its windows were covered with bars, until we were on our way to New York and Ellis Island.

Chapter Ten: *REFUGEES ON ELLIS ISLAND*

"There is a stubbornness about me that never can bear to be frightened at the will of others."
Jane Austen, Pride and Prejudice

Ellis Island gave us a very different welcome. Each of us was interrogated separately. Mama could not speak for me or be with me when I was questioned. Eventually we were assigned a room, which we shared with a single lady. Our room had six iron twin beds, tile floors, and white tile walls. The windows were located high up in the wall, too high to provide a view of anything but the sky, and they had bars on them. I wondered how long we would have to stay in this place that felt like a prison. On the second day we went through medical examinations, which included tests for tuberculosis. When we went back for the nurse to look at our TB test, she determined mine was positive. I would need to be taken for further exams. I sat alone on a cold chair swinging my legs back and forth, when a few moments later an attendant came in with a wheelchair to transport me through many long corridors to the hospital building. Along the way I glanced through windows to the outside. It was wonderful to see grass and trees, and I got a glimpse of the Statue of Liberty. After x-rays and more blood tests, I was put to bed in a hospital room. I wondered if Mama knew where I was. I wasn't given the opportunity to say goodbye to her. The nurse told me that if I had TB, I would not be permitted to immigrate. "What about my mother and sister?" I asked. "It will not affect them. They will be able to immigrate," she said. I wondered where they would send me, if indeed the x-ray was positive for TB. When fear raised its ugly head momentarily, I recalled how I had allowed fear to overwhelm me the night of Mama's great abdominal pain. I decided I was not going to descend to that hell of fear again. *I have a Heavenly Father who loves me, and I will be fine*, I declared to myself. I hoped Mama and Anna would still immigrate without me, because I would feel terrible to be the roadblock for our plans of starting a safe new life in America. The next day Mama and Anna appeared in my room. Mama looked so worried, I tried to reassure her that I was fine and not afraid. After one more day in the hospital, I was declared healthy and returned to our quarters.

Days dragged by. A few mornings a week they gathered the children to study English and American history. As unpleasant as Ellis Island was, nevertheless, in a strange way, I felt safer this far removed from the USSR. Mother was busy writing letters. She had contacts in Boston, Connecticut, New York, Washington, DC, and the church in Chattanooga, Tennessee. Week after week, month after month, permission to immigrate did not arrive. A Latvian friend who lived in New York obtained a one-day pass for us to visit her in the city, shortly before Christmas. New York decked out for Christmas, with light displays on every street, was an awe-inspiring sight after many months in one white tile room. The elaborate displays in store windows, with dancing figurines and chugging trains, were magical. We had a wonderful day touring the city. When we returned to Ellis Island in the evening, I thought surely by Christmas or soon thereafter they would set us free from Ellis Island.

Christmas arrived. Mama tried to make it special - she wrapped gifts in pretty handkerchiefs for Anna and me. Anna received a ring with an oblong topaz that was too big for her ring finger, but it fit her middle finger and looked elegant. I received a gold bracelet with an amethyst flower surrounded by seed pearls. We had nothing to give Mama. Downstairs in the gathering room of Ellis Island a Christmas tree had been decorated. On Christmas morning each of the children who were detained received a gift, which was probably provided by some charity. The gifts were wrapped in colorful Christmas paper, and I was excited to receive mine. I ran up to our room to show Mama. “Hmmff,” she said. “It's just junk.” She was right of course, although I disagreed, and I liked the pretty Christmas wrapping paper. Before lunch time, all the little plastic toys in my gift bag broke when I played with them, except for a paddle board. On Christmas Day, I went around hitting the ball, attached by a rubber band to the paddle, and wearing my new gold bracelet. I was very pleased with my gifts.

A year before we left Sweden, when Mama had gone to the American Embassy in Stockholm to check on the status of her visa application, she had learned about an organization that paired emigrant families to churches in America willing to sponsor them.

Every immigrant needed a sponsor - American hardworking taxpayers should not have the burden of taking care of foreigners if they were to fall on hard times and not be able to provide for themselves. Mama understood and completely agreed. That Christian organization had connected us to a church in Chattanooga, Tennessee that was willing to take on that responsibility. A Mrs. Keese was our contact person for the church, and the immigration officers in Boston had telephoned her and allowed Mama to speak with her. When Mrs. Keese learned that our Visa application had been lost at the US Embassy in Stockholm and we had arrived in America without a Visa, she went to work. She was a dynamic Christian lady of great faith. She contacted her United States senator, Senator Kefauver. Soon after arriving in Ellis Island, someone from Senator Kefauver's office came to speak with Mama. He explained that the Senator had initiated an amendment to a bill that had passed all the committees and with the cooperation of Congressman Armstrong from Connecticut, who would speak to Congress in support of the amendment, he believed it would go forward without a hitch. They had added this amendment to a bill that was ready to be voted on, and it stated that we, as stateless victims of WWII and Nazi aggression, may legally immigrate to the USA. When it passes both Houses President Truman would sign it. That would give us legal status and a green card to come to America. He thought it was moving very quickly through the halls of Congress. As we endured that incarceration I didn't think "quickly" was the right word. Looking back at that uncomfortable, boring time of waiting, a time laced with uncertainty, I realize that having the whole Congress pass a bill for the President to sign, which had to be done since it is illegal to arrive in America without a Visa, and getting it done in only five months, was a minor miracle. I am forever grateful to all the people involved.

At the end of January, we received the news that the bill had been signed by President Truman. We were elated! We each had one more interview individually with the immigration officials. "What do you want your American name to be?" the lady asked me. "The English for Katrina is *Catherine*. Don't you want to be an American girl with an English name?" I did not want to offend the official, so I said, "Yes." My legal name was changed to Katherine. I didn't want to change my name, and I never went by it.

Then she said as she typed, "you were born in Riga, USSR." "No, no I born in Latvia" I almost shouted. "There is no Latvia anymore; isn't it part of the USSR now?" "No, no, I born in Riga, Latvia" I insisted. I thought, *she can change my name to an American name, Latvians did that to foreign people as well, but she can't change where I was born!* She had to backtrack with her typewriter and fix, what I considered, to be a major mistake. After that we had our pictures taken for the green card. Days later we were free!

Chapter Eleven: *AMERICA*

"Freedom is the open window through which pours the sunlight of the human spirit and human dignity." Herbert Hoover

Our first responsibility was to take the train to Chattanooga, Tennessee, to thank the wonderful people who had sponsored us. I was healthy and strong and able to help on this train ride. There was so much to see along the way! In Washington, DC, we had to transfer trains. I was so excited to see people who had come from Africa up close. Mother told me not to stare. I thought of our friend who lived in the South African Bush. Before her husband joined her, the native people were her only friends. I hoped someday I would have a friend like that.

In Chattanooga we were met by Mrs. Keese, and she invited us to be guests in their lovely home. After Ellis Island, sharing one beautifully appointed bedroom felt luxurious to me. I slept in a lounge chair. I lay down and was enveloped in a garden of blue and white flowers. I didn't mind that my feet hung off the end, if I stretched out. Mama and Anna shared the large queen-size bed. Dinner was a treat for the eyes and the taste buds and culminated with Baked Alaska for dessert. Baked Alaska was something new to me, and I loved it. I was delighted when our hostess offered us a second portion. Mama had taught us that it wasn't polite to say "Yes" the first-time seconds were offered. Only when the hostess asked the second time, if anyone would care for more dessert, should I say, "Yes please." So politely I said, "No thank you," and watched the Baked Alaska disappear back into the kitchen. It was all I could do to stay in my seat and not run after it. I realized that I would be learning many new customs in America.

On Sunday we went to the Church that sponsored us. How does one thank people who extend the love of God to strangers? What thank you is enough for the trust they had placed in us by sponsoring us? Years later I would be able to participate in sponsoring a family from Vietnam and in that way pay it forward. In 1950 we were the ones in need of someone to trust us, to trust our desire and ability to become contributing members of the country that welcomed us.

Mama was surprised to discover that the ladies committee of the church had made plans for our lives in America. In sponsoring us they had to sign documents that they would be financially responsible for us if we should fall on hard times, so naturally they wanted to offer Mama job opportunities and show her possible living quarters. For my strong willed, intellectual, independent mother it was a very awkward situation. She did not think she was suited to work in the laundry and had every intention to become involved with a university up north as soon as her English improved. Nor did she want to be dependent on these kind people. Many telephone calls were made to the place in Connecticut where Mama wanted to be while we oriented ourselves to this new country. Eventually she was able to reassure the church committee that she knew what she was doing and that they did not need to be concerned or feel responsible for our financial well-being. A week later we were back at the train station with the ladies committee to see us off.

While the ladies talked, I decided to take advantage of the restroom before we boarded the train. I discovered a dilemma; there was a restroom with one sign that read *Ladies*, and another beside it that read *Women*. Which restroom should a girl use? *Ladies* or *Women*? I decided *Ladies* must be for my mother and grown-ups, and *Women* must be for girls, thinking that it was silly that they had not written *Girls* instead of *Women*, I went in. There were several girls and ladies inside standing off to the side. I thought the girls' mothers had accompanied them. I found an empty stall, did what I needed to do, then came out and washed my hands. I smiled at a girl about my age and was surprised when she said, "You're not supposed to be in here." I looked at her quizzically, obviously questioning what she said. "You aren't supposed to be in here" she repeated. I thought to myself, *You're in here. Why shouldn't I be?* as I exited. When the church ladies saw me emerge from the restroom, they all giggled and whispered to each other. I learned that there were separate bathrooms for African descendants. I had not read the word above *Women*, or maybe I didn't know the word *Colored* yet. In any case I thought it very strange and wondered why.

The home in Greenwich, Connecticut, which was our temporary residence, was an old mansion. Most of the bottom floor was rented out to a ballet teacher. The former ballroom had been transformed into a studio for her students. Handrails had been installed on three sides of the room and mirrors on two walls. The kitchen and an adjoining dining room were used by refugees resettled from the American zone in Europe. At the end of WWII, the Allies divided the war-torn countries of Europe into responsibility zones, and each member country was responsible to help rebuild their zone. Many Latvian refugees, who feared the Soviet Union because of their brutal occupation in 1940, followed retreating German troops into the western part of Germany, where they ended up in refugee resettlement camps. The woman who owned the mansion offered temporary housing to them after they were declared stateless refugees and brought to America. There were several Latvians living there, who shared with us all they had learned about life in America. Mrs. Cowan, the generous proprietor, was a most gracious lady. Her smile shown with the love of God. She was well established in Greenwich society, and with her many contacts helped Mama secure a job as a filing clerk in the office of a large company. Although Mama could read English very well, her accent was difficult for some people to understand. This job allowed her to earn an income while living rent-free and at the same time improve her American English skills. Mrs. Cowan arranged interviews for Anna and me at private schools. In the fall of 1951, Anna started the ninth grade at Rosemary Hall, and I entered the seventh grade at Greenwich Academy.

Mama had studied ballet from her youth. In college she was selected to perform with the Riga Ballet Company in their production of *Aida*, Papa's favorite opera. She had trained with a world-famous ballerina. When Mama discovered the ballroom of that old mansion, her face lit up. She volunteered to help the ballet teacher. After a few weeks of volunteering, Mama was offered a small stipend as an assistant teacher on weekends and evenings after she came home from work. All the while Mama wondered what she could do with her new degree in meteorology. She contacted several universities. She also contacted the Baroque School of Languages in Washington, DC, and the Library of Congress. At the University of Latvia when she studied library science, she had learned the Congress library system. The first responses she received to her applications were from the Baroque School of Languages in DC and the Library of Congress. The Library said they needed someone with foreign language skills. She accepted both jobs. By Christmas we were settled in a rented, furnished apartment in our new country's Capitol. Anna would continue her high school education in Connecticut, where she received a scholarship to become a boarding student. I was out of school again since the Greenwich Academy was only a day school.

In DC, Mama and I went to the Jarvis School Bureau. It was like a real estate office that represented private schools. After much deliberation and several interviews, we settled on a small school on the Eastern Shore of Maryland that accepted boarding students starting in the seventh grade. The headmistress allowed me to start school in January. I have blocked out the name of the school from my memory because, during my five months there, I learned what it felt like to be persecuted, bullied, and teased for being different, for being a foreigner. I didn't fit in. The highlight of those five months was that the school had as many horses as girls. Some of the girls had brought their own horse from home to the school. To get away from the girls, I spent every minute of my free time with the horse assigned to me. The single redeeming event of those six months was the horse show at the end of the school year. I, the outcast, and the horse I loved, received the reserve championship ribbon!

Chapter Twelve: *DISCOVERING A NEW HOME*

And we know that all things God works for the good of those who love him, who have been called according to his purpose.
St. Paul's Letter to the Romans Chapter 8 verse 28

The silver lining of that dark school experience was that, in the spring, Mama and I returned to the Jarvis School Bureau to look at other schools. I chose Sanford Preparatory School. My troubles at the previous school started during the Valentine Dance in February, just a few weeks after I arrived. The "queen bee" of the seventh and eighth grade girls became irate because, unknown to me, she had claimed for herself the boy who had asked me to dance. He then escorted me to the refreshments table and continued dancing with me. The previous fall, the boys' school had hosted the girls' school for the Fall Dance, and that's when she had developed a crush on that particular boy. There is no wrath like that of a "queen bee" scorned! I decided it would be safer to go to a school where boys and girls study together, so that the girls would not be so boy-crazy. I also wanted a school with horses. Sanford had both. Fortunately, Mama approved of their academic standing.

A few weeks after we had submitted our application, I needed to return to the Jarvis School Bureau for an interview to see if I would be accepted. Mama gave me money for taxi fare and went to work. I went to meet the Dean of Students, Nancy Sawin, by myself. She and I immediately developed a rapport, and I was accepted. I believe it was by the Grace of God. As I stepped off the train in Delaware, and was met by a driver from the school, he told me he was also picking up another student, **Dave Wilson**, who would be in the same class with me. When we met, I thought he was very cute. I tried to make polite conversation as we were driven to school; I discovered that he was very quiet. During that car ride, I had no idea that ten years later he would be the young man standing at the Altar in the Naval Academy Chapel, with his quiet strength, smiling at me as I was escorted up the long aisle to become his wife. I thank God for the mean girls at that first school, because if they had been nice, I might have stayed at that school and never met Dave.

The eighth-grade class at Sanford Preparatory School had fifteen students — thirteen boys and two girls. All the girls, from seventh through twelfth grade, lived in one dormitory. The school wanted the cultural diversity that foreign students brought. There was a boy from Persia in the ninth grade, whose accent was nearly as pronounced as mine. All the seventh through ninth grade girls tended to hang around together. One evening they said, "We need to give you a nickname. Katrina is too long, what would you like to be called?" "I don't know, vhat is a nickname?" I asked. The Latvian alphabet does not have a *w*. It was a year before I learned to pronounced *w* instead of saying a *v* where there was a *w*. They tried out several nicknames and finally decided that they should call me *Kitty*, if I agreed. "Nicknames," I learned a new word, my parents had nicknames for each other. Having the girls choose a nickname for me made me feel like one of them, so I readily agreed. Dorothy was *Dot*, Suzanne was *Sue*, and I was happy to be *Kitty*.

That year flew by. We had schoolwork until two or three in the afternoon, then field hockey in the fall, basketball in the winter, and lacrosse in the spring. Music classes included singing and learning an instrument. I chose to learn to play the violin.

When summer break arrived, I returned to Washington, DC by train. I had a trunk, a handbag, and my borrowed violin, so that I could practice during the summer. Mama was very pleased that I was learning to play an instrument. One day when she arrived home from work and heard me practicing, she came into the living room, and said, "Oh, very good, I am so pleased you are practicing. Keep it up — you're making good progress." Then she walked out, closing the door behind her. As her footsteps went down the hall, I heard every possible door close. The screeching sounds that I, a beginner violin player, was making while learning the fingering could set one's teeth on edge. All those doors closing told me I needed to spend a lot more time practicing if I hoped to be invited to play in the school orchestra come fall.

In the fall I returned to school early to prepare for hockey camp. I got off the train in Wilmington, Delaware, feeling confident. I was no longer the new kid. Bill Sawin met my train, and we went to pick up my trunk only to discover that it had not arrived. "No problem," the attendant said. Bill agreed and explained to me that when you check a large trunk, it is put in with cargo, which might be on a different train. He said he would check on it and come back tomorrow to retrieve it. I arrived back at school with my violin, handbag, and nothing else. My school uniforms, including sports uniform, hockey stick, lacrosse stick, books, and jewelry to complement party dresses, was in my trunk. Even the gold bracelet with the amethyst flower surrounded by seed pearls, was in the trunk. It had belonged to Ama, and I received it as a Christmas present when we were incarcerated in Ellis Island. It meant so much to me, every time I touched it, I thought of my Ama and the happy days of my childhood. Without my trunk I had to rinse out my underwear every night and borrow clothes from fellow students. That evening I inquired about my trunk and was told that it had not arrived yet. Day after day Bill checked for my trunk. A week passed, and my friends were growing tired of lending me clothes. I had become concerned. Another week went by with no news. I went to Nancy Sawin and said, "A big trunk can't just disappear! It must be somewhere. Could you please bring pressure on the railroad company to find my trunk?" She explained that she had already called more than once and requested that they search all the depots on the East Coast, and even train stations to the West, all the way to Chicago. "Kitty, you need to call your mother. You can't keep borrowing other people's clothes. You need to let her know what has happened." Nancy said. My heart started to race. The thought of telling Mama that everything she had bought for me was lost, even the bracelet that had belonged to my grandmother was lost, was unthinkable! She worked two jobs to provide for Anna and me to have this wonderful academic experience in a safe and nurturing environment. I recalled, when a check to Anna's school had been lost once, she had lived on oatmeal for a week until things were straightened out. No, I was not going to call my mother. I was going to pray about it. A trunk is a solid thing, and God sees everything. He must know where it is. A few days later, Nancy called me into the office to explain to me that the search had failed; I had no recourse except to replace everything I needed for the school year. She said, "I told them that you were not a student who could readily replace your belongings, and they assured me that they had contacted every depot on the East Coast and all the way west to Chicago as well. No one knows where your trunk is. What did your mother say?" I shook my head to indicate *no*, I had not called Mama. I didn't know what to say to her. "You must call her today," Nancy said firmly. I left her office distraught. With tears running down my cheeks I ran down the stone steps that led to the valley below on Sanford's large campus.

There in the valley was a little chapel. It was too small for any school activities and available for private prayer only. At first, I walked nervously up and down the aisle of the chapel. Then I noticed an album on a podium in the back of the chapel. I sat down and leafed through the book, and read other people's prayers, seeking inspiration. "Oh God," I said out loud. "I can't call Mama! I can't burden her with such a large financial problem, on top of everything she's doing for me. She has been through so much. She has lost so much. Now she lives to give Anna and me a normal life! I just can't ask her for more. What shall I do?" I looked up at the beautiful stain glass windows, the sun was casting lovely hues of blue light across the Altar, I arose from my seat at the back of the chapel and went forward to kneel at the Altar rail. "O God I don't know what to do?" My quiet weeping turned to wailing out loud. I reached up my hands and cried out; "Father in Heaven, you said you were going to be my father. Where are you now? Where are you? You know I love you. I trust you, Lord. I am your child. I always will be, but Lord, I can't burden my mother with this." I stopped speaking when big wails heaved out from my belly. It felt like a geyser of pain burst out. I was crying out loud, tears running down my cheeks, dripping onto the Altar rails. After several minutes of my lament, my heaving was interrupted by a comforting arm around my shoulder. I jumped up and quickly and turned around, I was horrified that someone had heard me bawling out of control. I was mortified; I felt embarrassed and self-conscious, ashamed that someone had discovered me bawling out loud. I'm not the only one who has ever lost a trunk. No one in America, no one who had not survived all I had would be able to understand what I was feeling. *What could I say to them*? I thought as I turned around. To my astonishment there was no one there. No one was standing behind me. My eyes scanned the whole interior of the chapel searching for whomever had put their arm around me. The chapel was empty, I was still alone in that little chapel. I was dumfounded; I had stopped crying abruptly out of embarrassment. Now what? I turned back around and thought of crying out to God again.

I had not heard his voice within me. I didn't know what to do. Nevertheless, a peace had come over me. I said out loud, "Okay, God, I don't understand nevertheless, I'm going to give it one more day even though Nancy told me I must call my mother today." *That's all I know to do*, I thought. I dried my face, blew my dripping nose, and left the chapel. I felt startled and peaceful at the same time with a wait-and-see attitude. Had an angel embraced me?

Back in the girls' dorm, I put a smile on my face, took a shower and prepared for dinner with the other girls. I was hoping to avoid Nancy, because I had disobeyed her and not called Mama. As we left the dorm, Nancy was walking right towards us. She called me aside, my stomach lurched, and I thought I was going to be sick. Then I noticed a lilt in her voice; it didn't seem like she was going to scold me again. She said, with a smile, "We received a phone call this afternoon. They have your trunk at the Wilmington Depot. Bill is driving in right now to pick it up." "Wow, where has it been for over two weeks?" I asked astounded? "I don't know," Nancy replied, shaking her head. "They simply said they had it. I wanted you to have the good news right away. You'll need to call your mother back." I laughed and danced around in a circle of joy. She laughed with me. I don't think she heard me whisper, "Thank you, Heavenly Father." I never had to call Mama.

Chapter Thirteen: *THE LOSS OF INNOCENCE*

But you, Lord, are a shield around me, my glory, the one who lifts my head. Psalm 3 v.3

Ninth grade was a year of change. Several new girls entered our school to join my class. It was a happy circumstance for me; I could be the one who already belonged and enjoyed welcoming them, helping them adjust to boarding school life. Another big change was that Mama was offered a job by the Harvard University Department of Meteorology to work in their Blue Hill Observatory. She moved to Boston. I felt at home at Sanford and didn't want to change schools. Anna was still in Connecticut and would be closer to Mama now. Mama wanted both of us to come to Boston for Thanksgiving, to become acquainted with her new town. On the Wednesday before Thanksgiving, I boarded the train for the long trip up the East Coast. Mama was waiting for me as the train came to a stop. It was a joyful reunion. It was so good to see her looking happy at last. She seemed to have less stress in her face, and once again she had a sparkle in her eyes. She was excited about her new job. Mama told me that a lady friend of hers had invited her to stay in their home while she was looking for an apartment. "We will be comfortable at Julia's. They never go up to their third-floor rooms," she told me.

Our taxi stopped at a large, beautiful Victorian house. I was warmly greeted by Julia and her husband. Anna had arrived earlier. It was wonderful to see her again, and she seemed so grownup compared to me. She was tall, beautiful, and of course I still envied her thick wavy hair. The formalities, required of us as guests, didn't give Anna and me much time to become reacquainted Wednesday night. On Thanksgiving Day, Julia and Mama prepared a sumptuous Thanksgiving feast, with a little help from Anna and me. We feasted in their spacious dining room. I felt a little nostalgic, recalling the festive occasions we had celebrated in Latvia in our beautiful dining room. It seemed to me that Anna and I had grown apart during our long absences, because she was treated more like an adult and I like a child. While we were still at Ellis Island, Anna and I had decided that we should converse in Swedish so we wouldn't forget the language, and now we had that opportunity. We could speak freely knowing our host family could not understand us. With Mama we would speak in Latvian. Our rooms were on the third floor. As soon as it seemed polite after dinner, we excused ourselves and ran up to the third floor to catch up and share stories from school. It didn't take us long to become reacquainted and start giggling like in old times when we lived together. We talked late into the night. The next day, Mama took us on a tour of Boston and showed us the apartment she would be renting. It was unfurnished, so for the first time since leaving our home in Latvia Mama would be acquiring her own furniture. She liked antiques and had studied a great deal about Oriental rugs while in Latvia.

Julia's husband was an elderly, gray-haired man. I found him very amusing, and he entertained me while Mama and Julia we're having a fun time chatting. They were planning their shopping trip for Saturday morning. Julia wanted Mama to help her choose a large Oriental carpet at an auction. She knew Mama would provide valuable guidance for this major purchase. On Friday evening, Anna left us to spend a day with a classmate, who would drive her back to school Sunday morning. Saturday morning mother whispered to me as I lay in bed, "We're leaving; go back to sleep. Sleep, sleep, you need to catch up on your rest," she said, as she tucked my sheets and blanket tightly under the mattress. I drifted back to sleep in my warm cocoon of bed covers.

The next time I woke up I was startled to see Julia's husband standing by my bed. "You're still sleeping?" he asked with a smile. "Young girls need a lot of sleep, I understand. You're growing into such a beautiful young girl. If your father were here, he would have many things to teach you. Would you like me to be your surrogate uncle and teach you things fathers teach their young daughters?" He sat down on my bed and started stroking my shoulder. I didn't like him talking about my father; he didn't know how wonderful my father was. He was not family, and he was making me feel uncomfortable. On the other hand, he is the husband of Mama's good friend and hosting us for the Thanksgiving weekend. Therefore, I needed to be polite so I simply said "No thank you." His hand moved down from my shoulder. *Hasn't he noticed that I'm developing breasts, and that it's inappropriate for him to have his hand go down my chest?* I frowned at him. I was a little confused as well as uncomfortable. I had been taught to respect elders, and I was a guest in his house. Could I ask him, please, to leave? *Maybe he isn't the nice old man I thought he was last night.* He kept smiling at me and giving me compliments. Suddenly he leaned down and tried to kiss me. I turned my head away. He moved his body right across mine, lying on top of me. He tried to pull back my covers. Now I was horrified, frightened and started to panic. "You better leave, you better leave!" I kept shouting, as I continued to move my head from side to side. Then he held my head in both of his hands so that I could not turn it to the side. He covered my screams with his mouth. I gritted my teeth tightly. He whispered, "Come on, give me your tongue." His tongue pressed hard against my teeth. When he moved a hand from my head in order to pull off my bed linens, I moved my head from side to side, screaming at the top my lungs, "Stop! Go away! Help! Help!" I held onto my sheet and blanket, which I pulled tightly up to my neck. He started to laugh and said, "There's no one in the house. There's no sense in yelling. There is no one to hear you." "Stop, go away!" I yelled feeling helpless. I was scared that I was about to be raped but I was determined to fight him with all my might. My sheet and blanket, which Mother had tucked under the mattress so tightly around me, were my only armor of protection. I held onto them with all my might as he tried to pull them down and out from under the mattress on the side. His weight on top of me in the twin bed must have kept the blanket securely tucked in. Then I felt his hand between my legs through the bed covers, which he had been unable to remove. I crossed my legs as he lifted up to unzip his slacks. His hands were moving all over my body. Whenever he let go of my head, I dared to release one hand from holding on to the covers so I could hit him and push him, all the while yelling, "Stop! stop!" As the battle went on, his eyes took on a shiny, devilish glow. He didn't look like himself anymore. How long we struggled I couldn't tell, and eventually he tired of fighting me. He stopped and got up with his private parts hanging outside his pants. He said, "Don't be a stupid girl and make up lies when nothing happened," he said over and over again, as he walked towards the door, "nothing happened." He looked at me with an angry scowl, zipping up his slacks. He jumped and exclaimed a little "ow" when his penis, still hanging out, got caught in the zipper. Then he repeated; "Don't you go telling any lies! Nothing happened. Nothing happened, foolish girl." Those were his parting words to me as he closed the door behind him. I lay motionless, listening for his footsteps walking down the stairs. Now I was a foolish girl, not someone he lathered with compliments. I had fought him with all my strength. All my adrenaline had drained out of me, and I began to shiver in fear. I was afraid to get up. *What if he comes back while I am getting dressed?* I thought. I decided to stay where I was until Mama came back. I reached down and tucked the covers back in tightly, where he had slightly loosened them. I laid there listening for any sound coming from the hall.

Around lunchtime I was relieved to hear ladies' voices downstairs. Mama came into my room, took one look at me, and said, "What happened?" Her smile vanished, replaced by concern in her eyes. She must have seen the fear in my face. I didn't want to be "a foolish girl," so I started to tell her what happened from the beginning. "I woke up, with Julia's husband standing by my bed…"

I only got as far as he laid on top of me. Mama's mouth dropped open, and she ran out of the room and down the stairs screaming. She was screaming at Julia's husband down on the first floor so loudly that I could hear every word. Soon Julia joined in screaming at him. They were both crying and screaming at him. I thought to myself — *I didn't tell any lies*. I very carefully began to describe what happened. I didn't even get to the part where he hurt himself with his zipper. I hoped it hurt a lot!

Mother understood that I would not want to see him again. The two of us went out for a nice evening. She explained to me that Julia had promised to take her husband to the doctor. He was going through the change of life, like women's menopause, and it had made him crazy. He was going to have to get on medication or be reported to the police, Mama said. I didn't care what happened to him, as long as I didn't have to look at him. I knew Mama also felt badly for her friend Julia. Her care and understanding for me was very healing. But I would never trust compliments again. In the war I have learned not to trust people — to be cautious about their motives. Now I became suspicious of older men. "Forgive us our trespasses as we forgive those who trespass against us."

When I told the Lord I could not forgive that man, a question occurred to me; wasn't it curious that as strong as he was, he was unable to pull the covers out from under the mattress?

It was a long time before I was able to forgive him. It was years before I even wanted to try to forgive. Through a church group I learned that unforgiveness is a heavy burden, which only hurts the one carrying it. It has no effect on the offender. I learned that forgiving an offender doesn't excuse their offense or crime. Understanding that is what enabled me to ask God to help me want to forgive him. It doesn't relieve a sinner from the consequences of their actions. Forgiveness is what God wants from us, and for us, so that we can be whole. Jesus, while suffering crucifixion said *"Father forgive them, they don't know what they are doing."* In prayer, I asked God to help me want to forgive him, and then the more I learned about Jesus' merciful and forgiving nature, the more I wanted to forgive others - including him.

Many years later when I heard he had died, I was surprised at the first thought that popped into my head; "he's burning in hell now." Wow! I thought I had completely forgiven, but obviously I had not. I went and knelt by my bed to talk to my Father. I know our Heavenly Father desires for everyone to come to repentance and receive His redemption and love. He sent his Son, Jesus, to die for our sins — a costly death. He spilled his blood to wash away all our sins - *all* our sins.

I want to have the mind of Christ. He would not wish anyone to burn in hell. He wants all of us to repent and turn from our sin, to receive forgiveness and the unconditional love of our Heavenly Father. **He will send us the gift of the Holy Spirit to help us live our life according to his Word in the Bible - all we must do is to sincerely ask him.** Without the power of the Holy Spirit to enlighten us, we can't understand the Bible or have the wisdom to resist the temptations that will accost us daily. The world seeks to pull us away from the good and satisfying life God wants us to enjoy.

"Forgive me Lord - and forgive him," I prayed. "I hope that he turned his life over to you and is not burning in hell, but is whole and healed," I whispered. Yes, I really wished that for him, and I realized I was finally free.

The emotional scars left by sexual abuse are subtle and can last a lifetime. One out of four girls, and one out of five boys experience some sort of sexual abuse trauma. I was fortunate and felt thankful for a mother who believed me and stood up for me. **Most of all I was fortunate to have a personal relationship with Jesus, who is our healer, comforter, and our righteousness.**

Chapter Fourteen: *GROWING UP*

Listen, my son/daughter, to your father's instruction and do not forsake your mother's teaching,
they are a garland of grace around your head and a chain to adorn your neck.
Proverbs 1:8-9

I was happy to return to school, and to reunite with all my friends. I never told any of them what happened to me — I was embarrassed and worried that in some way something about me was seductive. One of my new friends at school was Helen, whose family rented a large home on the edge of our campus. She was a day student. Many weekends Helen invited me to dinner at her home. While helping her mother with dinner preparation, the three of us would talk nonstop, like three friends. I learned a lot about American cooking from Aunt Betty, as Helen's Mother invited me to call her. For instance, I learned spring corn needs to boil for only five minutes. It was delicious. Mama had bought corn at a farmers' market the previous summer. At home she said to me, "Corn is a starch, like a potato. These large ears of corn probably need to boil for forty minutes." When we tried to eat the corn, it was awful. Sticky kernels became glued to our teeth, and after one bite we threw them in that trash. Mother said, "That's why in Latvia we only feed corn to the animals." Helen's Mother, Aunt Betty, laughed when I told her that story. Helen became my best friend, and her home became a second home to me.

I love dancing! Sanford, as a coed school, hosted three or four dances every year. A committee of students and teachers would decorate the hall, and the school prepared the refreshments. The boys were instructed to invite girls for a dance, and all of us were encouraged to dance with many partners so no one was left out. In ninth grade, after a few dances with different people, Dave, the cute classmate I met the first day I arrived in Wilmington, asked me to dance after the required mixers, and then stayed by my side for refreshments and dancing the rest of the evening. After the final dance, he asked if he could escort to me back to the girl's dorm. Outside the dorm, called Steven May, there was a wide, low fence on both sides of the sidewalk. We saw several couples sitting there.

Dave sat down on the fence and took my hand. I stood in front of him as we continued our conversation, lingering in the pleasant moment. The first bell sounded, alerting students of the upcoming curfew. I said, "I guess I better go in." Dave said with a smile, "Yes, I suppose you have to." He put his hands on either side of my waist and drew me closer. Our smiling eyes met, and he leaned forward, his lips touching mine. I responded, my eyes closed to the warm, moist, velvet touch of his lips. As we drew apart from my first kiss, a string of saliva stretched between his lips and mine. I took another step backwards, feeling shy and embarrassed at seeing the saliva still connecting us. As I took the step backward the string of saliva stretched but did not break — it had to be twelve inches long by then! At that point, both of us broke out laughing instead of being embarrassed, and I took my hand and swiped it halfway between us, not wanting to wipe my lips. I wonder sometimes, with a chuckle, if that was not a prophetic sign? We have often laughed tenderly about the memory of our first kiss.

Dave and I didn't become boyfriend and girlfriend at school. We thought we were too good of friends to be boyfriend and girlfriend. Besides, he was a year and three months younger than me, which for some silly reason mattered in high school. We enjoyed each other's friendship and the many opportunities we had to work together on projects including the student court, and the student council.

Sanford School was situated outside the city of Wilmington on beautiful farmland with rolling hills and flat field where cattle and horses grazed. Tall pine trees and whitewashed fences lined the road to the various buildings that comprised the school. It was a lovely location for summer camp when school was not in session. The camp was open to children from grades one through junior high. I applied to be a camp counselor. I wanted to help the equestrian instructor. I had learned to ride, how to take care of horses, clean their hooves, wash them down, and curry their fur at the school I attended in Maryland for five months. My application was accepted. I was provided room, board, and a small stipend for the summer. I was thrilled. Since camp started only ten days after the end of school, I asked Mama if I could stay in Delaware. Helen and her family had invited me to go to Rehoboth Beach with them. Helen and I were like two peas in a pod, we had a fabulous time swimming, sunbathing, or boating every day. In the evening we walked the boardwalk, checking out all the cute boys.

Back at Sanford, my job as camp counselor didn't feel like a job at all. I enjoyed working with the horses so much. I think they could sense that I loved them, and they responded to me. I learned to understand all the different personalities of the horses. For instance, one horse whose name was Champ, was too hard for a twelve-year-old to handle, but he was gentle, patient, and very cooperative when a little first or second grader was on his back. He was the horse I rode. All the counselors got along well. We had much more freedom than I had during the school year. We were able to go off campus when not working. I decided to apply to be a counselor at Camp every summer. I grew two inches taller that summer. Anna could hardly recognize me when I went to Boston for a short visit after camp.

The rhythm for my life in school was set. For the first time since leaving Latvia I experienced stability. In the fall I went to school ten days early for field-hockey camp. I stayed at school through the short Thanksgiving break until Christmas. Then I took the train to Boston to celebrate Christmas with Mama and Anna. I was back at school for the spring semester, a drive to Rehoboth Beach with Helen and her family, followed by work as counselor at summer camp. I went back to Boston for about two weeks before returning to school. For five years I saw Mama and Anna for approximately four weeks a year.

My senior year was my fifth year as a boarding student at Sanford. I had been elected senior gavel girl, and as such I had responsibility for the girls' dormitory. The house mother was merely an adult presence — the girls went to her for a kind ear to listen, or for help with sewing on a button or mending a zipper. The gavel girl was responsible for the proper and timely functioning of the dorm. She had to make certain morning and evening bells were sounded at the correct time, that rooms were kept in order, and Saturday morning jobs assigned and fulfilled properly. If a teacher saw a student dancing in a common room downstairs on Sunday, instead of addressing the problem herself, since dancing on Sunday was not permitted, she found me. I was to tell them they had to stop. I had the power to give demerits, and as members of the student court, the gavel boy and girl had the power to recommend dismissal of students, in consultation with the administration, of course. It was a lot of responsibility and pressure. In May of my junior year, and every May at Sanford, classes were suspended for a day called "gavel day." The student body was to consider who in next year's senior class had exemplified the leadership qualities needed to be their gavel girl and gavel boy. After the votes were tallied and the names announced, there was a big celebration. Now that I was doing the job of gavel girl, however, I often found myself between a rock and a hard place. If the students weren't angry at me, a teacher or the dean of women was. Besides all that responsibility I carried, I needed to decide which university I would like to attend and what I wanted to study after graduation. I did not want to burden my mother with any more large tuition payments.

For many years, really since I had been that small sickly child, I had wanted to be a dentist. Now I thought about how many years of study that would require. It seemed daunting, especially when I thought of the expense of tuition. My friends teased me and said, "Why would you want to have your hands in strangers' mouths? That would be yucky!" If I was not going to apply to prepare for dental school, I didn't know what I wanted to study after graduation. That was very unsettling and sometimes I felt bewildered. My dear friend, Dave, had been elected captain of the football team. In one of our first games, he was brutally hit by a lineman twice his size, which resulted in a torn cruciate ligament in his knee. The surgery to remove the damaged ligament was scheduled to take place on his birthday, October the 25th. Dave had no family in town to comfort him. He had told his parents that it was not necessary for them to come all the way from Colorado. Helen and I requested a day pass from school to go visit him in the hospital. She, as a day student, could drive us. It was a chilly fall day, and I wore my red wool dress with a mink collar. The mink Mama had sewn on the collar was some she had salvaged from her Latvian fur coat. It still looked beautiful. Helen and I walked into Dave's hospital room shortly after his surgery. He was groggy from anesthesia, having just been brought back to his room. In a slurry voice, Dave said, "Aren't you a sight for sore eyes, in that red dress." Helen and l laughed; we were happy that the timing for our visit had been just right. We felt so badly that he did not have any family there to comfort him. After visiting with him for about an hour, we could see he was drifting off to sleep, we left him with get-well cards, flowers, and candy and tiptoed out.

During my Christmas vacation that year I needed to catch up on some homework. I poured out my heart to her mother, explaining to her how very stressed I felt. Sanford had been my stable home for almost five years. I found my emotions in turmoil at the thought of leaving, and I felt overwhelmed and exhausted with all the work I had to do as gavel girl. The class work for seniors was heavy, and the uncertainty of my future after graduation was even a heavier burden. I started to cry as I described all my concerns to her. I said, "I have so much work to do as a gavel girl and I have this 10,000-word paper to write, and I don't know what I want to do after I graduate" I rattled off one concern after another. "It will be alright. You will do it, one project at a time," she tried to reassure me. "Oh Mommy, can I sit in your lap one last time? I know I'm too big. I just want my mommy's lap." She opened her arms, and I got in her lap. I couldn't curl up like I did when I was a little girl, but it was strangely comforting. She put her arms around me and in a quiet, gentle voice reassured me, while stroking my head and rocking me gently. My tears dried up and peace returned. After a few minutes, I got up and laughed at myself. "I hope I didn't hurt your legs," I said.

Anna had eloped the previous fall, because Mama would not hear of her getting married prior to graduating from university. She was living with her husband in Boston. They invited me to a New Year's Ball, but I felt conflicted about the invitation. I didn't want to leave Mama alone on New Year's Eve and secondly, I wouldn't know anyone at the party except Anna and her husband Gene. Mama wanted me to go; "Go have some fun, meet some young people who live and study in Boston." She said, "I was young once; now it's your turn. My parents had seamstresses make beautiful dresses for me in Latvia from imported silks in the latest Paris styles. As a student in Latvia, I enjoyed many wonderful Balls. Go have a good time". I could see that resurfacing memories lit up her face with a smile. I smiled as well and agreed to go. "I was young once, now it's your turn," she said again nodding her head.

Before I left for the evening, Mama had me turn around in a circle. "Ah ja, that looks just right," she said smiling, her lips pursed. I was the only high school student mingling with Anna and Gene's college friends but it didn't seem to matter, my self-consciousness soon vanished. A friend of theirs, who joined our table, was a very good dancer, I had a fabulous time dancing nonstop. About a minute before midnight, Anna and I gave each other a nod; we had decided that we would call Mama at midnight. We dashed out of the ballroom to find a wall telephone; there were no cell phones in the fifties! Anna held the receiver of the telephone close to both of our ears so the three of us could greet each other, as we welcomed 1957.

A few days later Anna invited me to go with her and a group of students for pizza in Cambridge. I enjoyed the best pizza I had ever tasted. The conversation was lively and interesting. They discussed current events and political ideologies. I felt too intimidated to open my mouth. I did not enter into the conversation until they were discussing the need for affirmative action. One of the guys said; "we need affirmative action, because people of African descent don't have the intellectual capability to compete academically. It's the only way we'll be able to get some diversity among doctors, or policemen, or many other professions." I had felt that as a high school student, I couldn't compete with their cerebral banter. However, after that outlandish statement I thought I would burst if I kept my mouth shut. I vigorously entered the debate. I had studied American history and thought that I understood the root of prejudice in the US. That it existed among Ivy League students in the late fifties, was shocking to me, and I thought that young man was an intellectual snob. "Oh, I'm not prejudiced," he said. "I think they're outstanding people. I appreciate the great athletes and actors they are." I responded, "Yes, a high percentage of Americans of African descent are superior athletes, because "the survival of the fittest" means that a physically weak person could not survive the slave ships. But that does not mean they are less capable intellectually." I had gotten really hot under the collar. As I recall, he changed the subject rather than admit that a high school student could get the better of him in the debate. I think his faulty thinking was mostly due to the history books available to students. Our books at the time did not include any intellectual accomplishments of African-Americans. In the letters we received from Mama's friend, who lived in South Africa, I had read about the wonderful and bright people with whom she worked.

My visit to Boston was a happy time. Seeing Anna happy, visiting with her so frequently, and being with Mama, of course. I made the decision that after high school I would move to Boston, live with Mama, study, and work part time so she would no longer have the burden of large tuition payments. The decision made, I returned to school with a clear purpose and peace of mind.

The Senior Class at Sanford had many responsibilities. We gave the talk, or sermonette, at the weekly chapel service. My turn was coming up. We also had a ten thousand word paper to write, and we had to memorize and recite the entire poem, "The Rime of the Ancient Mariner" by Samuel Coleridge, which is his longest major poem — about six hundred lines. On top of that, I had the job of gavel girl, along with all my other homework. The first assignment I tackled was to prepare my talk for chapel. I chose to speak on 1 John 4:15-18, and couple that to John 3:16. More than one classmate had used the beautiful reading from chapter thirteen of First Corinthians, often called the 'love chapter,' or the Twenty-third Psalm. My talk was about love as well, but I included John 3:16, to explain that love is very costly and sacrificial. I had certainly seen the sacrificial love of my parents, but in Jesus' sacrifice; He obediently fulfilled the will of our heavenly Father and said yes to the cross, yes to taking our sin upon himself so we could be blameless, clothed with his righteousness in the sight of Holy God, that was Ultimate Love. "*There is no love without surrender and sacrifice*, I wrote. The desire to call forth the best in each other, to see the best in one another, is a demonstration of love in action. The exciting and fun feelings of falling in romantic love is like cotton candy — it may look pretty and taste sweet for a while, but it shrinks down to nothing unless we put love into action. *Think of Jesus on the cross as your example of love*, I wrote. Since I had tasted the love of God, I sincerely wanted to convey the depth of His love without talking about my personal experience in the Baltic Sea, when we had to escape from the Nazis and Communists. That experience of Jesus was still my guiding North Star, the plumb line for my life and my secret. "For God so loved the world that he gave his one and only Son, that whosoever believes in him shall not perish but have eternal life" (John 3:16). That is BIG love.

When I got up to give my speech, at the front of the auditorium filled with the whole student body and all the teachers, my knees were literally knocking against each other. I thought my voice would quiver. Writing my speech was the easy part — would I be able to control my voice to deliver it? I looked down from the podium at all my fellow students and thought, ***God loves each one. Think about Him, not my performance or message. Just convey His love to them,*** I told myself. Shifting the focus from myself to them and what God would want them to hear made all the difference. I felt better as I began to speak. I made it through just fine despite my quivering knees.

At the end of the last semester, Dave and I decided we would keep in touch by writing letters once a month to each other. We exchanged addresses. When the yearbook came out, I sought out all my classmates, wanting them to write something of significance in my yearbook. Dave wrote that before I got married, he wanted to meet the guy so he could give his approval. I laughed and responded that I would definitely want to have his advice!

Mama came to graduation. It was the first time she had visited Sanford, which had been the first place that provided stability and felt like a home to me since our escape from occupied Latvia. My classmates had been like family to me. I had grown and become very independent. I escorted mother around the campus with pride, and she began to understand the significance of terms like "gavel girl" as they were applied to me. She was getting her very first glimpse into my life, as if through a kaleidoscope. I was no longer the sickly, weak link in our threesome. I had written to her once a month while in school, but we had lived separate lives for five years. By now I spoke English with barely an accent, I spoke my native Latvian with an accent instead. I had forgotten how to speak Swedish altogether unfortunately. I looked forward to relearning Latvian and life with Mama, as I bid a fond farewell to all my classmates and teachers.

Chapter Fifteen: *SURPRISED BY LOVE.*

When I Fall In Love It Will Be Forever
Song written by Edward Heyman and Victor Young

Mama had arranged for me to shadow a friend of hers, Dr. Zarina, who was working in medical research in Boston. She had her PhD and oversaw hospital laboratories, along with working on her own medical research project. I knew I had found my calling when I observed her work throughout the day. During my senior year at Sanford, I had abandoned the goal of becoming a dentist. What I liked about dentistry was that it involved both the mind and the hands, and one did not sit behind a desk all day. Work in a laboratory fascinated me — it involved the brain, the hands, and asking questions.

I have always been an inquisitive person. Even my questions have questions! Medical research was the field I was born for. Dr. Zarina told me about a new program Harvard had initiated that provided training and study simultaneously. That sounded wonderful; I applied and was accepted. In the fall, I was happily engaged studying pathology, cytology etc. etc. I studied regular college classes in the evening. I was as happy as a clam working in my lab, interested in everything I was learning and thirsty to learn more.

Through my sister I met several Latvian students, and I joined a Latvian sorority called *Dzintras*, or Amber in English. Dating in the 1950s was fun. I might go to dinner and a show with one young man on Friday night, and Saturday go with a different student to a football game and after-party. The idea was to get to know someone before becoming serious and dating one person exclusively.

At work, a young doctor doing his residency rotation in pathology, started to come into my lab for coffee. He kept asking me out. I had seen Teddy at a party come out of a bedroom with a nurse he was dating at the time and I noticed her dress was partially unzipped in the back. I had lost respect for him and decided he was a "player". I was not interested in accepting his invitations. He assured me he was no longer dating her and kept coming to visit me in my lab. I got a kick out of his persistence and started looking forward to his visits. After a couple of months, I relented and accepted an invitation to go with him and a group of interns to the beach. We had a good time and afterwards I felt safe to accept an occasional invitation to attend a party or dinner and a movie with Teddy. I thought I could convert him.

Dave, after a year at Colorado University in Boulder had transferred to the Naval Academy. We had been corresponding by mail ever since our graduation from Sanford. I was happy to read that Dave would be back on the East Coast. He was required to attend the United States Naval Academy for four years, even though he had successfully completed a year of studies in Colorado. The first year at the Academy is the called "plebe" year, and the midshipmen are not allowed to date. His first letter from the Academy explained the challenges of plebe year, and he wrote that he didn't want to read about my dating problems anymore. I had been seeking his council in some of my letters. At the end of his plebe year Dave had a brief summer vacation. First, he visited his family on the ranch in Colorado, and then he caught a military flight to Boston to surprise me and visit Nick, his Naval Academy roommate. Unfortunately, the surprise was on him as I was at the Cape with my mother. Dave kept calling our home with no response. There were no cell phones or answering machine in the fifties. I returned home from the Cape late Saturday night of Labor Day weekend to repack my suitcase and drive to New Hampshire for a party on Sunday evening with some of my sorority sisters. As I unlocked the door, I heard the telephone ringing. I rushed inside and picked up the receiver. What a delightful surprise to hear the familiar voice of my dear friend Dave. "Hi Kitty, this is Dave." "Dave, hi! What a nice surprise to hear your voice, where are you?" "I'm in Newton, Massachusetts, I am staying with my roommate Nick. I've been calling you all weekend, where have you been?" "You're in Massachusetts and you didn't tell me you were coming?" I exclaimed. "I've been at the Cape with my mother; if I'd known you were coming, I would have stayed home to see you, or you could've come out to the Cape for a day." "I wanted to surprise you, I guess that wasn't such a hot idea, was it?" We both laughed into the phone. I was sad that I had missed his visit to Boston. It was already late on Saturday night, "What are you doing tomorrow morning?" I asked. "I fly back to Annapolis in the afternoon, but if you're free, do you want to meet me for lunch at the airport or someplace nearby?" "Yes" I said enthusiastically, "let's meet at the airport, it is not far from the highway I need to take to New Hampshire." It was decided, we would meet at the airport before his flight back to Annapolis. We could spend a few hours together, have some lunch and have a good visit at one of the restaurants in the airport. I had planned to wear a red flowery cotton dress to the party in New Hampshire. As I put it on, the next morning, I recalled how much Dave liked the red dress I wore when I visited him in the hospital after his knee surgery and I smiled to myself.

When I got to the airport, I spotted Dave right away. He was wearing his white Navy uniform. I took one look at him and thought to myself, *Wow! My friend has grown up. The cute boy is now a handsome man!* I looked into his beautiful hazel eyes, sparkling and so earnest. We opened our arms to each other, and I thought as we embraced, *here is a man, true, with no guile.* Our reunion was warm, and comfortable as only close friends can know. We freely shared about our lives and the few hours we had together flew by. As I walked Dave to the gate for his flight, he invited me to come to the Army vs. Navy football game. I said, "Sure. I would love to go! I can't wait to see you again now that you're on the East Coast." We gave each other a friendly hug and smilingly said, "See you in November".

At the time, I had no understanding of the big deal an invitation to the Army vs Navy game was. The game had been played between the two Academies for almost one hundred years. The pomp and circumstance surrounding the game involved traditions from the very first game. Most years, the President of the United States is present and spends half of the game on the Army side and half of the game on the Navy side, marching across the field at halftime.

After that first date, I began to make the long drive to the Naval Academy in Maryland monthly for a game or a formal ball or just because he invited me. As the end of that school year approach David invited me to come for "June week" and mailed to me a schedule of events. As I read over the activities and planned my wardrobe, I became more and more excited. A week with Dave sailing, swimming, picnicking and watching him in a parade and of course dancing was a lot to look forward to. When June finally arrived the week with Dave in Annapolis exceeded my expectations. It concluded with a formal Ball. The schedule had allotted two hours of free time to get ready for that special evening. The girls, who shared the rented house with me, and I had a lot of fun and lots of giggles as we helped each other primp. I wore a floor length, strapless, sheath gown with a slit in the back. It was blue silk overlaid with blue lace. The men arrived, dressed in their formal uniforms and patiently waited to escort us to the Ball as we helped each other zip-up our dresses and hurry to meet our dates.

In the white marble ballroom of Bancroft Hall music from a live band greeted us. I felt transformed to a fairyland in that exquisite hall. After dinner, the band began to play all of our favorite music from the late 1950s. We danced the jitterbug, the twist, and the cha-cha. It was while dancing the cha-cha that the trouble occurred. My stockings were held up by a garter belt. Attached to the garter belt with a hook were four stretchy straps that fastened to the stockings. As I turned with the rhythm of the music, I felt a hook come undone and slide down my abdomen. I froze momentarily but then kept dancing until I felt the hook of that same stocking pop off at my back. Now the weight of the hooks, at the end of the elastic straps, were pulling my stocking down. I stopped and whispered to Dave, "I'm in trouble!" He looked at me quizzically and I explained while standing still in the middle of the dance floor, "my stocking came undone and is sliding down my leg." "Come on, I'll escort you downstairs to the ladies' room," he calmly responded. We walked slowly out of that Grand Hall, I was taking little baby steps, and arrived at the top of wide marble stairs. By this time my stocking was wrapped around my shoe. I took one step down and both straps with the metal hooks clanked loudly against the marble steps, drawing the attention of everyone present. I froze again. Dave merely chuckled. He took my arm and with a grin on his face said, "don't look down, hold your head up and smile and keep walking." With smiles on our faces, looking as if nothing was wrong, we descended the 10 or 12 steps, accompanied by the click clack of my swinging garters. Back and forth they were clanging on the marble steps behind us and in front of us until we finally reached the lower level. I think maybe that's when I fell in love with Dave. His steadfastness and calm under pressure was so reassuring. After we returned, to the dance floor I was happy to hold him tightly as the band played a slow romantic ballad. Dave smiled at me and asked; "How would you like to wear my pin?" I wondered what that meant. Was he asking me to date him exclusively as my boyfriend? My inability to trust people accosted me. "How many girls have you given that thing to?" I asked in a light-hearted manner. "I just received it this afternoon," he responded. "I'd like you to be my girlfriend but we don't have to date each other exclusively. If you want to go out with the other guys that's okay as long as I'm number one. He smiled. I felt embarrassed for my untrusting nature and told him I'd be honored to wear his pin.

When Teddy learned about my trips to see Dave, he teased me and called the Naval Academy "the boat school." I was a little smitten with all the attention coming from Teddy but I respected Dave more. Teddy and I talked a great deal about my faith in God. I so wanted him to come to have a personal relationship with Jesus. One day he said, "If you believe that God created us, then he created us as sexual beings, so we should not repress our sexual desires." I responded, "Yes, he did create us as sexual beings, and there is a lot written about sex in the Bible. It clearly tells us that sex is the consummation of the union between husband and wife. In marriage they give their bodies to each other as a wedding gift." "Well, when we are married and have a daughter, I'll send her and a nice boy to the barn on her eighteenth birthday if not before," he said laughing. "Not my daughter, you won't!" I retorted. But then I decided to challenge him from, what I thought was a medical point of view. "You know that the very essence of who we are as human beings exists in our DNA. The body fluids released when two people make love mingle, and become as one. The man and woman become one, their secretions become one DNA sauce, even if an egg is not fertilized by sperm, that's serious," I said seriously. "One DNA sauce, hmmm?" he said and started to laugh. "I've never heard it put that way. How romantic." I went on, not willing to be distracted. "The Bible says, 'a man shall leave his father and mother and cleave to his wife, and the two shall become one flesh.' What do you think that means?" Without giving him a chance to answer I continued. "I think it's talking about our DNA. Wouldn't you agree?" He tried to humor me out of my serious mood by putting his arms around my waist. He whispered; "When I kiss you, I know you want to go further, I think you are repressing your desire". Now it was my turn to laugh, as I pushed him away, I said "don't flatter yourself." "Besides, 'repressing' is the wrong word. God expects us to exercise self-control because as you said 'He made us sexual human beings' so we should trust that he knows what is best for us in the long run." "Is that right?" he asked, his smile fading. "Besides right now, you are distracting me from my work." Now, many years later, I smile as I recall the youthful understanding I had about the meaning of the "oneness" of a husband and wife. In Christ it is so much richer than I understood at the time. God has truly blessed me to know that oneness of heart, mind, soul, and body as my husband and I have lived united under the authority of Christ. I recently heard Dave counsel a young couple. He said, "Neither of you is perfect, only Christ is perfect. You will both disappoint each other at times, so my question is, do you believe you are perfect for each other? Are you willing to let Christ be the head of your household and let Him teach you how to love and live out the covenant you are entering into? Are you willing to choose to love when you are disappointed and in a disagreement with each other?"

Less than a year after the brief reunion Dave and I had at Boston airport, I was no longer dating Teddy or anyone else. I had no interest in going out and staying up late no matter how glamorous the occasion. The only one I wanted to see was Dave. I had returned home from spending a wonderfully long weekend with Dave in Annapolis, and the realization struck me that I was in love with my best friend. *Oh God,* I thought, *this is terrible, I have fallen in love with Dave. I don't know if he loves me seriously or just likes me a lot as a friend.* Romance could ruin our long friendship if it didn't work out. Dave's friendship meant so much to me, I was willing to suffer a broken heart rather than lose his friendship. I didn't have a dad or brother, but I'd had Dave's warm friendship since I was thirteen. I got down on my knees by my bed and prayed. I told the Lord how much Dave has meant to me for a long time, and now I was in love with him. What should I do? Should I stop dating him to preserve our friendship? "Oh Lord, my precious Holy Father, what should I do?" I asked. I travailed in prayer because I didn't want to risk losing Dave's friendship. **Finally, I heard, in my head, "*Do you want to control your future or trust***

Me?" "Okay, Lord, I trust you. I will not try to figure out the future. I will go with the flow, one day at time." I climbed into bed with my peace restored. I had trusted God in the past, and I would trust him with my future. I would not stop dating Dave. A few months later, when Dave came to visit me in Boston, he asked me to marry him. We drove home to tell Mama. I was so excited, and I thought she would be too. I expected her to break out the champagne chilling in the refrigerator. When we told her our exciting news, however, she looked at Dave very seriously, raised one eyebrow, and said, "Nu? I don't know about that. How do you think you will be able to support my daughter on the salary of a young officer?" I was totally caught off guard. Practical things like that had not entered my mind, and it did not matter to me - we were in love! Besides, all I had lived through had taught me that material things are not the source of our happiness. I said, "Oh Mama, let's celebrate. Let's get out the champagne and have a toast!" "Well, well. I don't know about this," she said again, shaking her head, even as she turned to go to the kitchen for the champagne. We would not be able to get married for a year and a half, since midshipmen were not allowed to marry.

David's parents had a very different response when they received news that I had accepted Dave's proposal. I had briefly met both of his parents at our high school. His Dad and I had spent a lot of time together on the weekend of Dave's twenty-first birthday. Mr. Brownlow Wilson had to fly East to New York to meet the publisher of his book and had arranged that meeting for October, to coincide with the week of his son's birthday. Dave procured tickets to a Navy football game in Philadelphia for us, and he asked me, if after the weekend in Philadelphia I would drive his dad up to New York for his appointments with the publisher.

On Friday of Dave's birthday weekend, I drove to Philadelphia, checked into the hotel, and freshened up for the dinner party. Dave's parents were British. His father was born in Saint Andrews, Scotland. I recalled seeing the cliffs of Scotland as we sailed from Sweden to America. I had been told that his father had attended the British Naval School as a classmate of Lord Mountbatten. During the Second World War he was called back into the British Navy and stationed in San Francisco as the liaison officer between the

US Navy and the British Navy. I was more than a little apprehensive to be spending so much time alone with a staid Scotsman. As I descended the stairs at the hotel to meet Mr. Wilson, there he was, standing near the bottom of the stairs waiting for me. He recognized me from photographs and smiled up at me, and I noticed he was wearing a bright red tie. I thought to myself, "*Anyone who would wear a bright red tie can't be too stuffy.*" Dave's father was most entertaining at dinner, as he regaled us with stories about ranch life and his time in the Navy. He told us that during the First World War he was stationed on a destroyer patrolling the North Sea. In a storm, a wave had swept him off the deck into the frigid ocean (one doesn't survive more than a few minutes in water that cold) and the next wave lifted him back up to the ship and a ship mate extended a hook to him and rescued him. Dave's friends, all midshipmen, were mesmerized by his adventures in the British Navy. After the first World War, Mr. Wilson received a medical discharge. Apparently, his heart had been damaged when he was swept into the North Sea. He told us that he was devastated by that news, "I had envisioned my life as a career naval officer, I went home to Saint Andrews feeling at a loss." "My sister, Doris, said 'Brownlow, stop moping around, go to America and learn the ranching business, that would be a help to Father.'" Their father owned a large ranch in New Mexico. My response was, "What would I do out there? I don't know the front end of a cow from the back end!" All of us at the table laughed at that statement. He continued; "Doris wouldn't let me feel sorry for myself, she said, 'it's high time you learned.'" "That was the best thing she could have said to me. Our father owned a ranch in New Mexico, and I came out here in the 1920s thinking that I would be here for a few months, but I fell in love with the ranch and the beautiful, rugged land."

The WS ranch, owned by his father (Dave's grandfather), encompassed 125,000 acres. Mr. Wilson started off working as a cowboy under the supervision of their ranch manager. He had to learn to ride a Western saddle, rope cattle, manage all the cowboys and learn the breeding program. I could just imagine how many practical jokes the cowboys played on him, a tall, lanky redhaired Brit with a funny accent. "Oh yes, they did! I could receive it and I could give it right back to them; it was all in good fun." I asked, "did you meet Mrs. Wilson in America?" "No, on a visit to Scotland. I courted her and convinced her to join me in America."

We were fascinated with his stories about life on the ranch, about the life of a cowboy and his hunting adventures. Sometimes I could not tell if a story was a joke or an actual happening. He told us about encountering a mountain lion on a narrow ledge. "There was a steep drop off to my right and a cliff rising straight up to my left. I was face to face with the lion. Then the lion crouched and leapt at me. I punched my fist right into his mouth so hard I could grab his tail and pull him inside out. Problem solved - now we were going in the same direction!" I was wide-eyed and sitting on the edge of my chair until he said; "I punched the lion in his mouth and grabbed his tail and turned him inside out!" Laughter erupted at our table again and again. Dave's dad was a lot of fun, telling his jokes and stories with a straight face, none of us were in a hurry to leave the table. The dining room was nearly empty when we finally arose.

The next day, after the football game, Dave had to return to Annapolis. I drove his dad to New York as planned. I enjoyed his company and invited him to come for dinner. Brownie, Mr. Wilson had told me to call him by his first name, had mentioned that he loved steak and kidney pie, a Scottish dish. With help from my roommate, I baked the unfamiliar dish. Brownie loved it! About a week later I received a thank you note from him. After the appropriate expressions of appreciation, he wrote, *I'm looking forward to having you in the family.* At that time Dave had not yet asked me to marry him; he had asked me to wear his pin, but he hadn't proposed. Therefore, when we became engaged it was not a surprise to the Wilsons. Brownie said he would be honored if I called him Dad. Dave's mother was Mykie to everyone, and I loved them both dearly.

One year after our engagement, Dave and I became unsettled. I was thinking to myself, it's easy for someone to love me when dating and having a good time, going to football games, parties or the theater, but will Dave continue to love me when I'm tired and just not at my best? The thought of giving myself to one man for the rest of my life was frightening, I would be giving up my independence. I decided that when Dave came to visit for a week right after Christmas, we should see if we can be happy just "hanging out." We would be celebrating the New Year together, about five months before our June wedding. After we get married, we will not be able to afford tickets to theaters very often, or dinners in fancy restaurants where we can go dancing, on an Ensign's salary, as my mother had pointed out. With those thoughts in mind, I didn't plan any special parties or outings for his visit. It didn't go well, and both of us felt badly after that visit. Were we ready to enter into the commitment of marriage? When Dave got back to Annapolis, he called me and asked me to come down as soon as I was able, so we could have a serious talk. I agreed that that was needed and was important. Two weeks later Dave and I sat at a quiet corner table in one of the little restaurants in Annapolis, talking about marriage and how we envisioned our life together as a couple. Dave said, "I think if we want to have a good marriage, we will need to keep Christ in the center and have a Christian marriage." The previous fall Dave had volunteered to be the 13th Company's representative to the Officers' Christian Fellowship. As he entered his first meeting of the OCF he was greeted by a classmate, A.J. Egerton, who soon asked Dave, "When did you come to know the Lord?" I was taken aback — that's not how Anglicans talk. AJ said to me, "You need to be sure you have a personal relationship with Jesus. Come by my room and let me show you some scriptures." "I said, 'I'm pretty busy;' but afterwards I thought about it. AJ was just as busy as I was — all Midshipmen had the same schedule."

As Dave continued talking, he pulled out a piece of paper from his pocket, unfolded it so I could see, and continued with his story. "After contemplating AJ's invitation, I decided I needed more Christian grounding if I was going to be a good husband and a good officer. I went to AJ's room at 1730 (5:30pm), and AJ got right down to business — we only had about twenty minutes together. He took out this piece of paper and drew the picture of two cliffs with a chasm between them and explained that it was impossible for anyone to get from one side to the other on their own. Then he wrote down a Scripture verse from Romans 3:23, which reads: 'All have sinned and fall short of the glory of God.' "Then he asked me, 'Do you believe this to be true?' I acknowledged that I knew it was true. Then AJ wrote another Scripture verse on the same side of the chasm from Romans 6:23, which reads: 'For the wages of sin is death, but the gift of God is eternal life in Jesus Christ our Lord.' AJ was beginning to get my attention. He drew this cross between the two cliffs and wrote another Bible verse right on top of the cross from 1 John 1:9, which reads: 'If we confess our sins, he is faithful and just to forgive us our sins and purify us from all unrighteousness.' He then explained that the only way to get from one side of the chasm to the other is through the cross. Finally, on the other side of the page he wrote one more verse from Romans 10:9, which reads, 'If you confess with your lips that Jesus is Lord and believe in your heart that God raised him from the dead, you will be saved.'" I looked at the paper Dave was showing me, and I looked at Dave. He had never talked like this before. I knew this to be true and I was impressed. Dave continued, "I left AJ's room with this piece of paper that I'm showing you, and after I pondered the significance of what I had been told I knew I wanted to read those verses in my own Bible. Later that evening I pulled out my King James Bible. I went over all the verses and thought, this is much too easy." He looked from the paper into my eyes. I kept his gaze, surprised and puzzled, yet happy. I didn't know what to say, so I waited for him to continue. "There's a Christian bookstore in town, owned by a Naval Academy graduate, Jim Wilson. I went to see him, to see if it was really that easy to be sure I had a personal relationship with Jesus. I want to take you to meet him." "I would love to meet him," I said. "You have done a lot of soul searching since New Year's." "Yes, I have," Dave said. "We are getting married right after graduation, and during Christmas vacation we became concerned and unsure, right? The bottom line is I love you. I know you love me, and we both love Jesus. I believe, with His guidance, we can have a good marriage." "Yes Dave, I agree," I said, hope rising in me. He went on. "When I went to talk to Jim, he was great. He confirmed that it was that simple to ask Jesus into my life. He guided me through my prayer right there in the store. I asked God to forgive me, forgive my self-centeredness, etc. I thanked him for loving me so much that He would die for me, and I told him I want to have a personal relationship with Jesus and let Him guide my life by the Holy Spirit." I looked at this new Dave. He was so happy, so committed. For some reason I couldn't quite understand, it was a little scary to see the change in him. He was a new man, but he was also the same man I had fallen in love with. What Dave told me I knew to be true, but somehow his fervor and joy in sharing it was unsettling. I knew the Lord, I had a personal and secret relationship with Jesus, but I didn't have the Biblical knowledge to explain the plan of salvation as clearly and concisely as he had. I think that's what made me uncomfortable.

My mother always said, "Religion is too personal to talk about," when I tried to ask her about her faith. I had told Dave that I had a profound experience with Jesus, and that I trusted God more than myself or anyone. But I had not told him the whole story. I didn't want to talk about our escape or the arrest of my father. Whenever I recalled the glorious face of Jesus and His love washing over me, I disassociated that heavenly moment from the "hell" that was going on around me. I suspect that's why I was not comfortable telling anyone why I loved the Lord. As we walked to the bookstore, it was hard to explain what I was feeling. Maybe it was like a can of vegetables or sardines would feel, if it had feelings, when the sharp edge of a can opener is stuck in it and it is about to be opened, revealing what had been hidden inside. Jim greeted Dave like an old friend. I stood back, like always a little suspicious of people I first meet. Then Jim addressed me. I saw the same zeal in him as he was talking that I had seen in Dave when he showed me the scriptures. Jim wanted to pray for me to accept Jesus as my Lord and Savior. Dave spoke up. "She has a personal relationship with Jesus." Jim asked me, "When did you ask Jesus into your life?" That question made me nervous. After a moment I responded, "He came to me when I was in distress and I called for him to save me." "Do you remember when that was? You need to be sure." "Yes, I am sure. I was six," I said. I thought to myself, *how could I forget*? **Why did I know to call for Jesus to save me? I believed He could. I had been raised in a Christian family, baptized by my uncle, the Dean of Dome Cathedral in Riga, and Apap's devotion to our Lord had made an impression on me. From the moment that Jesus heard my desperate cry and came to me I have had a personal relationship with him.** Then Jim prayed with us, right there in the store. Jim Wilson was full of the love of the Lord — he enjoyed talking to the midshipmen, having been one himself. I think he gave away more books than he sold. I learned that day, that what Jesus said in Matthew10:27, I must live out. "What I tell you in the dark, speak in the daylight; what is whispered in your ear proclaim on the rooftop."

After that weekend of deep conversation, our minds were settled and our doubts vanquished. We made an appointment with the chaplain, which was required before he would agree to officiate at our wedding in the Academy Chapel. Joyfully we told him how deeply we were in love, (secretly I thought that we shared the deepest, strongest love of anyone ever in the history of the world and therefore we didn't need pre-marriage counseling) nevertheless as required, we attended all the required counseling sessions.

In the ensuing years we recall some of the counsel we received in those sessions with gratitude, after all, the upbringing Dave and I had experienced, before boarding school, had been so very different. Therefore, our approach to raising children was not similar, and could easily have caused serious conflict between us. However, in the euphoria of being in love, his statement that "being in love is part of the early stage of a marriage, living in love- that takes work," did not compute at the time, we were overflowing with love and longing for one another. With great joy we looked forward to, not only our wedding day, but our marriage, the life of a husband and wife with Christ at the helm.

Finally, the day arrived - June 7, 1962, our wedding day. We had celebrated all the fun of June week with Dave's family present, then the pomp and circumstance of a Naval Academy graduation. Now I stood at the back of the long center aisle of the Academy Chapel. Upfront, beneath the large, lovely, stained glass window depicting Jesus walking on water, stood my future husband, my friend, my love. He was flanked by the Navy chaplain in the center, with his brother Douglas and a row of classmates in summer white dress uniforms. Left of the chaplain stood my sister Anna, the matron of honor, then Dave's sister, Wendy, who had been my friend from our Sanford days, and my dear friend Helen. I wanted to run up that aisle to Dave. I was nervous. Nevertheless, I controlled my nerves to walk forward slowly in time with the music, nodding at our friends and family who had traveled long distances to be with us in Annapolis. After touching my mother's hand as she sat alone in the front pew, I looked into Dave's smiling eyes. We pledged before God and the gathered community "...to love and to cherish each other until death do us part." We were pronounced husband and wife.

The honeymoon for the two of us, two people who had refrained from expressing their love in physical intimacy, was a delightful feast of passion and a joyful celebration of our love. We couldn't get enough of each other, and because Dave did not have to report for flight training until mid-July, we had a whole month to make up for lost time. It was not just a vacation - it was a true honeymoon.

Seven years later, when Dave was in seminary studying to become a minister, he was required to study theology, ancient history, Greek, and Biblical exegesis as well as psychology. One night when the two of us were sitting in bed reading, Dave, reading his psychology book interrupted me with this question; "if we were flying in an airplane and I asked you to step out on the wing to bring me a cup of coffee would you do it?" "Of course, I would," I said with a laugh, assuming he was the pilot of the airplane. "In this chapter on human sexuality I am reading, it explains that when two people have come to trust each other so completely that they know whatever their spouse would request of them would be good and never, ever, harmful, then their sexual intimacy will be deeply fulfilling. I am happy to hear that you trust me that much," said Dave with a smile. "Completely!" I responded smiling back at him. I closed my book, and turned off the light and snuggled up to him.

June 7, 1962 Wedding at the Naval Academy Chapel

Chapter Sixteen: *A NAVY WIFE - 1962*

"Let every nation know, whether it wishes us well or ill, that we shall pay any price, bear any burden, meet any hardship, support any friend, oppose any foe to assure the survival and the success of liberty." John F. Kennedy

After five glorious weeks together, without responsibilities or separations, it was time for Dave to report for flight training. The drive from Colorado to Pensacola, Florida, took us through Mississippi and Alabama. For most of my time in America I had lived in the Northeast and had heard many untrue stories and jokes that were derogatory of the policemen in the South. Whenever Dave exceeded the speed limit by even a little bit, I tensed up and became anxious, telling him to slow down. I was concerned that behind the next row of shrubbery a policeman was waiting to give us a speeding ticket, and then he would take us to jail to extract a lot of money from us or our parents. I was relieved when we finally crossed the border into Florida. I exhaled and relaxed into my seat. Pensacola, a small town on the Gulf Coast of North Florida, was to be our first hometown. We drove to the home of one of our dear friends and Dave's former classmate. Neil had started flight training a few weeks earlier, and he and Peggy were a good source of information about good locations for rentals in Pensacola. We studied a local newspaper and read all the ads for rentals, and found a little two-bedroom cottage, unfurnished, for $65 a month.

"Let's go and purchase some furniture right away, at least the bedroom set, so we can spend the first night in our own home?" I asked. Peggy told us about a couple of furniture stores just off Main Street, and off we went. We didn't shop around — we bought the bedroom suit and had it delivered the same day. It served us well for forty years. What a thrill to spend the first night together in our own home! After a weekend of exploring Pensacola, with its powder-white sandy beaches and warm water, Dave checked into the base for orientation. *I am a stay-at-home housewife, what a novelty,* I thought to myself. I got busy unpacking boxes of wedding presents and arranging furniture my mother had donated, setting up our home. I wanted Dave to come home from his first day at the base to the aroma of dinner cooking. About a week after we settled into our first home, Dave arrived home with several legal forms to fill out. He was required to make out a Will and discuss it with me, his new bride. Back in Boston, I had been accosted by fear the day Dave told me he had passed his eye test and could go to Navy Air instead of submarines. He immediately canceled an appointment to meet with Admiral Rickover for an interview to enter the nuclear submarine program. He was so excited and happy; he had wanted to fly since high school. I, on the other hand, had been relieved that his eyesight was not good enough to enter the Navy's flight program, thinking he would be safe under the sea, under storms, in peace time. After he told me he was going Navy Air, I cried half the night. I had prayed for God's peace about Dave's decision, but I had been unable to trust God and be released from my fear. Now I was confronted with that same fear. Dave had to discuss his Will with me in case he was killed during flight training. He tried to assure me that it was just a formality, but I knew that Navy pilots received hazardous duty pay for good reason. Dave was as happy as he could be, the academic work was easy for him, and flying was a thrill. Soon he was flying solo, first in a single-engine and then a twin-engine airplane. We celebrated at the Officers Club the day he landed solo, without an instructor, on a Carrier. I was pregnant, nevertheless, I toasted his achievement. It was very reassuring for me to have his senior officers, his instructors, tell me what a great pilot my husband was. *A good pilot is a safe pilot,* I thought.

Now the decision before us was - what's next? What further training would he progress to? He told me he really wanted to fly jets, in which case we would move to Corpus Christi, Texas. I cried again. Flying jets seemed like the scariest, most dangerous choice he could make. I did not stand on the rock of my faith. Instead, I listened to the negative thoughts rumbling around in my mind. My Dad had died when I was young. Now my husband was going to be in danger, and our little baby might not have a Daddy. While reading Navy magazines, I learned that Sikorsky had developed a new, large jet helicopter. I showed the article to Dave, and said, "Here is a jet you can fly - a newly developed powerful jet helicopter. I think you'd be so much safer closer to the ground." Dave read the article. It piqued his interest, I think, not only because he had seen my fear but also because his last eye exam had not been the 20-20 result then required for jet pilots. I was thrilled when he decided to investigate that new helicopter. He later decided to learn to fly helicopters.

John Kennedy was president of the United States of America at the time. I had met him at the Army vs. Navy game in 1961, when during halftime he came across the field. Before he sat down three rows in front of me, he had greeted me and everyone who had the good fortune to be seated so close. In 1962, a few months after Dave and I were married, Khrushchev, of the Soviet Union, decided with Castro's permission to ship rockets and rocket launchers to the Island of Cuba, which is only about 123 miles from Key West, Florida, USA. President Kennedy ordered the U.S. Navy to blockade Soviet ships from entering Cuban waters. Dave learned his classmates were involved in the blockade and felt restless that he was continuing to study while his classmates did something concrete to protect America. I knew how much my people in Latvia were suffering under Communism, and I was extremely thankful and proud of President Kennedy for his strong stand against the encroachment of Communism into the Western Hemisphere.

In the fall, after Dave completed his training in Pensacola, we moved to Milton, Florida, where he began flying a more powerful single engine plane, the T-28. One day, shortly after we had settled into the officers' quarters on base, Dave burst through the door with a very serious expression on his face. He said, "Turn on the television! Have you heard? President Kennedy was shot!" That was unimaginable news. The President of the United States of America had been assassinated. Everyone was glued to the television, trying to digest the details of that tragedy. It will always and forever be a dark day in America's history.

In church one Sunday, the sermon was about putting God first in your life, based on the Greatest Commandment, "to love the Lord with all your heart, mind and soul." As I listened, I felt convicted. *I don't think God is my number one love. I love Him, I am in awe of Him, and I respect and worship Him, but I love Dave more*, I thought. Could there be something wrong with that, I wondered? During the prayer time, I whispered, "Lord, you know I love you. I stand before You humbly, daily grateful that You revealed Yourself to me. I love You, but I love Dave even more. I don't think you mind, since you gave him to me, do You?" Within the year I learned I had my priorities backwards. God, and God alone, needed to be number one — Dave and my children could be a close second. I am so grateful that our Lord is so patient with us and so forgiving. Getting my priorities straight helped me deal with the fear of losing Dave as I had lost my dad. Living with fear and negative expectations is like having faith in a bad outcome rather than in God. The fear I was dealing with, because of having lost my dad in WWII, was the opposite of the peace, joy, and faith God wanted to bless me with. I invited him to be number one in my life and asked for his help to live that out.

Our first daughter was borne in the spring at the little local hospital. We named her Kristina; it means Christ bearer. We were so excited and thankful as we held our beautiful, bruised baby, we were too happy to be concerned about the staph infection that she was diagnosed with by the pediatrician the next morning. The doctor who delivered her had put his brown leather shoe up on the delivery table and asked Dave to hold me by my armpits to keep me from being pulled off the table as he used forceps to forcefully deliver her. Because the Navy hospital was more than an hour drive from our home, we utilized the civilian hospital. The little local hospital was very good. Unfortunately, we did not know that the obstetrician who delivered our precious baby would soon lose his license to practice medicine. Both baby and mommy needed many months to heal after that traumatic delivery.

In the fall Dave received his Navy Wings of gold and orders to report to a base in San Diego California.

Chapter Seventeen: *VIETNAM - MY HUSBAND CALLED TO SERVE IN WAR*

"The Lord has promised good to me, his word my hope secures;"
From Amazing Grace by John Newton

Our first duty station was near San Diego, California, at Coronado Naval Air Station. Dave was assigned to the Yorktown, an anti-submarine warfare carrier. He deployed on two seven-month cruises and several short cruises after months of training in the new Sikorsky jet helicopter. After Dave checked in at the Navy Base, we contacted the Officers' Christian Fellowship representative and got involved in a Bible study. When Dave was at sea, the members of the Bible study and the wives of the squadron, understood the adjustment required of a family for the long absence of the husband and dad and knew how best to support one another in practical ways as well is loving thoughtful gestures.

During the second seven-month cruise, I was pregnant with our second child. One night, while I was sleeping soundly, I was awakened in stark terror. I knew in my mind and heart that Dave was in trouble and that I needed to pray for him, but I was too panicked to know what to pray. I jumped out of bed, grabbed my Bible from the nightstand, got on my knees, and turned to the ninety-first Psalm. I prayed the Psalm, inserting Dave's name in each line. "Whoever (Dave) dwells in the shelter of the Most High (he) will rest in the shadow of the Almighty. Dave will say to the Lord, 'He is my refuge and my fortress, my God in Him will I trust. Surely, He shall deliver Dave from the snare of the fowler and from the deadly pestilence. Dave shall not be afraid of the terror by night nor of the arrow that flies by day." Etc. About two-thirds of the way through the Psalm, my anxiety was replaced with peace. I said, "Thank you, Lord. Thank you, Lord. I know all is well." For good measure, I continued to pray the Psalm to the end, inserting Dave's name. "With long life I shall satisfy Dave and show Dave my salvation." That's the last verse of Psalm Ninety-one.

Before I climbed back into bed, I wrote down the time and the date of that experience, then I went back to sleep and slept soundly the rest of the night. I had purchased tickets to fly to Japan in a couple of months, to meet Dave when his ship docked in Sasebo Japan, for maintenance. I didn't want to forget the exact time and date of that experience so we could discuss it. I wanted to know what Dave was going through when I was awakened to pray for him. For days I continued to ponder the experience I had that night — it rumbled around my brain. I had no way of contacting Dave to ascertain what had happened. Every time I thought about it, I was flooded with a deep sense of gratitude for the Officer's Christian Fellowship Retreat I had attended a couple of weeks earlier. How fortunate that I had accepted the invitation from our OCF Bible study group to attend the areawide retreat. I had almost demurred, I didn't feel like going by myself without Dave. Even though it was a long drive up in the hills east of San Diego, I had "put on my big girl pants" and gone ahead. If I hadn't gone, I would have missed the opportunities to hear a British General tell the story of his experience visiting a young soldier in the hospital near the end of WWI. He told us that a soldier, who had been shot in the arm and torso, showed him his prayer book. It had a bullet hole in it, but the bullet had turned and exited the book before the page on which was printed the Ninety-first Psalm. That page didn't receive a scratch. His mother had written in the prayer book that she would pray the Ninety-first Psalm for him every day. He kept the book in his breast pocket over his heart, and it had protected his heart from a fatal bullet. If I had not gone to that retreat, I would not have known to pray that Psalm for Dave in the moment when I didn't know how to pray. But I went, and God used it to inspire me to pray that night.

Our reunion in Japan was blissful. Dave had booked a room for us in the Officer's Club. It was a beautiful old building - it had previously served as the Japanese officer's headquarters. It was the very building where the Japanese had planned the attack on Pearl Harbor. That was a sad and sobering thought, those awful decisions to attack Hawaii and kill so many people were birthed in the building that we were going to sleep in. We went up to our room and said a prayer that our Lord and Redeemer would fill our room with his love and peace. After that I didn't think any more about the evil schemes that had been planned in this lovely building. Dave had been granted ten days of leave, so we were free to be tourists and travel around Japan, learn about their ancient culture, and enjoy many beautiful, stylized gardens. We had a wonderful time - time to talk and reconnect. The sheer joy of being together after a long separation caused me to forget all the questions I had for Dave. One morning when we were reading the Bible together, that little note I had written, with date and time on it, fell out of my prayer book. I explained to Dave that I had been awakened abruptly and knew I had to pray for him. He calculated the time difference and looked at the calendar and then explained what happened. "I was assigned a copilot who had recently checked into our squadron. We didn't know each other, and I trusted he was well trained and experienced in night flying as it was a pitch-black night. Our mission was to search for a submarine. After taking off from the carrier and flying to the area of the Pacific where the Russian submarine had been spotted, we descended to one hundred fifty feet above the ocean. We slowed down and turned into the wind, then descended to hover forty feet over the water. The crewmen let down the sonar dome into the water to detect the location of the submarine. After a few hours of tracking the submarine, I turned the controls over to my copilot while I wrote up the exercise on my knee pad. As I was writing I felt a nudge to look up at the control panel, at the radar altimeter. I was shocked to see the helicopter descending straight toward the water. I grabbed the controls from the copilot, pulled up on the collective pitch control seconds before a tragedy would have occurred. I tell you, after I got the helicopter under control, I sent up quick prayer of thanks!" "Me too! I was awakened to pray for you," I said.

"I have always trusted my copilots, but if I had not looked up from my writing at that moment, it would've been too late. That would've been the end. We were picking up speed, going straight down, and that was not the only dangerous mistake he made that night. I found out that another pilot had written up his mistakes and said he wouldn't fly with him at night ever again. He had been assigned as my copilot to give him one last chance; I wish I'd been pre-warned. After I wrote out what happened, the guy was reassigned out of our squadron to safer, daytime only flying somewhere else." "Praise God that you are safe, I will continue to pray the 91st Psalm for you," I said and told him all about the OCF retreat I had attended.

After ten glorious days together, it was hard to say goodbye. It would be another three months until Dave would be home. Then our baby would be born, and Dave would rotate to shore duty — no more long cruises for a while. Dave escorted me to the train station before returning to the ship. I kissed him goodbye out in public at the station in Sasebo. The Japanese people never show affection out in public, but I didn't care about customs at that moment, I wanted to taste him, to breath him in, to feel his arms around me one last time before I boarded the train for Tokyo. When I arrived in Tokyo, I caught a taxi to the airport. I still did not understand Japanese money so I held out my hand full of Japanese coins to the taxi driver. I knew he would only take what I owed him for the fare and would not accept a tip. After boarding my flight, I collapsed into my economy seat happy and tired. The flight took me to Hawaii, where I was to transfer planes for my flight to San Diego. By the time I landed in Hawaii, I was having uncomfortable abdominal cramps and feeling exhausted. I spoke with a stewardess, who took one look at me and did not think I should board the flight home to San Diego. She rebooked me for a flight the next day and arranged for me to stay in a nearby hotel. Despite being in beautiful Hawaii, as soon as I got to my room I collapsed into bed and slept for twenty-four hours. I was almost six months pregnant, and I did not want to lose my baby in Hawaii. The next afternoon I returned to the airport and continued my flight home. To my surprise I had been upgraded to the business class. Back home in California, the doctor prescribed bedrest, which was a challenge with a three-year-old to take care of.

One night the phone woke me up from a sound sleep. Our home was a townhouse with two telephones — one a wall phone in the kitchen, the other one sat on a little table on the landing of the staircase between the first and second floor. Noting that it was after twelve at night, I was immediately concerned, plus I didn't want the ringing of the phone to awaken our three-year-old. I darted down the stairs to the landing and grabbed the phone, wondering what day it was. An unfamiliar male voice said, "Hi Katrina. Dave wouldn't want you to be lonely while he's off doing the government's dirty work. I'll be right over and show you what a real man can do." Not wanting to acknowledge that Dave was gone, I said, "He is napping. We were both sleeping, and I will report you to the phone company." I hung up. I had heard that people protesting the Vietnam war were harassing military personnel and their families. Now I was one of their targets. How had they learned my husband's nickname and his whereabouts? I wondered. I decided to try to make them believe they had incorrect information, so I insisted he was not away on a seven-month deployment. But that didn't stop the late-night phone calls. It was surprising and uncomfortable for me to hear how much he knew about Dave, whose first name is Harold in all the Navy files. This person knew Dave's nickname and about his deployment. I told my neighbor about the harassment. She was a kind, and mature lady. She immediately took these threats seriously. She said, "The next time he calls, keep him on the phone and come ring our doorbell. My husband will get on the phone and give him a piece of his mind." "The calls came at odd hours late at night," I told her. "I wouldn't want to wake you up." She replied, "He would be more than happy to go and get that harasser off the line. He would consider it to be his patriotic duty." It was decided.

A few days later the phone rang just as I had just gotten into bed. I grabbed my bathrobe so that after answering the phone I could go next door for my neighbor, then I ran down the half flight of steps to the landing where we kept our phone. I picked up the receiver and yelled into the phone with a gruff, nasal voice. "Hello!" After a moment of silence, a familiar voice said, "This is Captain Sommers. I'm so sorry to have bothered you at this late hour. I must have gotten the wrong number." "Oh, Al," I responded. "I'm sorry I answered the phone so rudely. I've been getting these nighttime calls harassing me about Dave being in Vietnam, so I wanted to sound like an old hag. Where are you?" "I am just back from Vietnam myself. I have a layover in San Diego and took a chance to call you and Dave. We heard over in Nam that wives were being harassed by protesters. That really makes me mad. I'm so sorry! I guess that means David's overseas. How are you doing?" "I'm doing fine, trying to stay quiet to keep our second baby from arriving too early," I said, feeling happy to be talking to an old friend. Al had been a classmate of Dave's and a groomsman and sword bearer in our wedding. After a nice chat I relaxed and went back to bed.

Every time I got up to run for the phone, I could feel my abdominal muscles contract and the pain return. It was May and the baby was not due until the tenth of August. I was already four centimeters dilated. Ann, a friend from our Bible Study, came to be with me for a part of every day to care for Kristina, so I could lie down in bed. One day the contractions did not stop even after I had been lying flat in bed for a few hours. We started timing them, and although they were not close together, they were quite regular. Ann decided to call my doctor, over my protests. He said I needed to be in the hospital and ordered an ambulance to transport me immediately. I could not ask Ann to take care of Kristina full-time. Thankfully Dave's mother, Mykie was able to come and stay with our three-and-a-half-year-old and relieve the friend who had stepped in to take care of her. I warned Mykie about the late-night phone calls. "Maybe you should unplug the hall phone when you go to bed so it won't wake you if it rings late at night," I suggested. Mykie was sixty-six years old and not very agile. I did not want her to get hurt. "I shall take out my hearing aids. If the telephone rings it won't bother me after we are in bed," she said with her customary laugh, setting my mind at ease.

In the hospital, I was kept on complete bed rest. I wrote letters to Dave almost every day, but I did not tell him that I was in the hospital and that his elderly mother came from Colorado to take care of Kristina. I did not want him to know about that because he would worry about us and worry could interfere with his concentration. The kind of flying he did required 100% concentration on the task at hand; there was no room for error. His squadron had been transformed, and their new mission was to search and rescue downed pilots as the Vietnam war intensified. I didn't want him to be concerned about his family. To be worrying about me and our baby might interfere with the "on purpose" concentration that was required for the dangerous flying he was doing.

Mykie had never learned to drive. In California you can't get anywhere without driving. Our friends took turns driving Mykie and Kristina to visit me in the hospital and our neighbors took her to the grocery store anytime they were going. All the wives from the squadron were very attentive as well. They brought me flowers and magazines, and it was always interesting to hear any news they could share. After several days of lying flat in bed in the hospital the contractions stopped, and I was allowed to get up to go to the bathroom. Mykie was a hero taking care of her unhappy three-and-a-half-year-old granddaughter who could not understand why her mother could not come home.

"Katrina, have you heard your husband is a hero?" Susan and Jan gushed as they came into my hospital room one June morning. "Oh no! What did he do? He's not supposed to be a hero - he's supposed to come home to me safe and sound," I blurted out before thinking. Even as the words left my mouth, I regretted them. That statement revealed that I still feared for his safety. I had grown a lot in faith and prayed the words of the Psalm 91 regularly. Yet. there it was, my first reaction had been fear, even before I asked them to tell me what happened. They became concerned that they had upset me and briefly told me that he had rescued pilots while under heavy fire. He was back on his carrier, and he was fine, they said. "All's well," said Susie. "Don't worry, it was great," said Jan.

"Lord, I believe; help Thou mine unbelief." I thought to myself, as I prayed a prayer of thanksgiving. My first reaction had been fear. *I am slowly learning to trust You. You promised me to keep him safe and he is. I praise You for your faithfulness, my Lord and my Heavenly Father.* Then I asked them for any details they knew. I wanted to know all about it. Years later I would be able to read a write up about the rescue.

Chapter Eighteen: *DAVE UNDER FIRE*

"You will not fear the terror of night, nor the arrow that flies by day" – Psalm 91:5

Dave, as commander of a large Sikorsky helicopter whose call sign was Fetch53, was in route to transfer a sailor from the aircraft carrier to a destroyer and deliver some classified material to another ship. As he flew north, close to North Vietnam, he heard a "May Day" call. An A6 Intruder aircraft had been shot down, the pilot and navigator had ejected, and the pilot was able to get out into the water, close to shore off North Vietnam. He was in the Gulf between Vietnam and the Island of Hon Matt, near the town of Vinh. Dave responded to the May Day call and ordered his crew to put on their bulletproof vests. He told the young sailor being transported to get down low, since they didn't have a bulletproof vest for him. Dave told me that the young man, on his first helicopter ride, turned white as a sheet when the crewmen opened the doors and tested the machine guns. Then he dumped some fuel to lighten the chopper and enable it to fly faster. They turned west towards land, flying low and as fast as possible. As they neared the shore, they could see an intense gun battle in progress. At least six A4 Skyhawks, a small, fast one-pilot jet, and several A1 Skyraiders had been called in to engage the guns on the beach and protect the downed pilot until the chopper could reach him. They were then to draw fire away from the slower moving chopper. That area off the coast of North Vietnam was known to be heavily fortified, with a lot of anti-aircraft guns and anti-aircraft missiles on the mainland, as well as on the island of Hon Matt.

Dave and his crew searched the water as they flew toward the coast. They spotted the pilot immediately, but they also spotted a fast, small gunboat, which was rapidly approaching the downed pilot. Thankfully an A4 pilot had seen it as well and sent bombs at the watercraft, which then retreated. The downed pilot was still under heavy fire. As the helicopter approached the pilot bobbing in the water, the gunners on shore turned their anti-aircraft guns towards the approaching helicopter. With the bullets and rockets whizzing past the helicopter from both directions, Dave had only one major goal in mind - it wasn't safe for him to think of anything else. He had to descend and move toward the downed pilot until he was nearly above him. When under fire, this procedure had to go right the first time with no do-overs. The wind swirled, causing the yellow rescue harness, referred to as a "horse collar," to blow around. Dave descended slowly, keeping his eyes and mind on the job at hand and not on the shoreline, where plumes of sand were exploding high in the air from artillery being fired and returned by our aircraft flying above him. Dave was able to guide the horse collar right up to the injured pilot's chest, praying that his injury wouldn't prevent him from getting in the harness. The second his crewman gave him the thumbs up, that the downed pilot was safely in the hoist and was efficiently being brought up, he moved to get out of the range of all the artillery coming at them. They had been sitting ducks for about thirty seconds. However, they had not spotted the downed navigator of the A6 Intruder.

The damage the helicopter received from the anti-aircraft fire didn't seem to be critical or affect safe flight. *Thanks be to God*, I thought as I read the report. Unfortunately, one of the A4s flying above him, while engaging the heavy fire coming from the beach, got hit and plunged toward the ocean in flames. The pilot successfully ejected from his burning airplane, and Dave and his crew saw the parachute and that the pilot skillfully released it, landing in the water of the Gulf of Tonkin. This pilot, fortunately, landed further from the shore, but he was still within range of rocket fire. Dave flew to his aid as he bobbed in the warm gulf water. Approaching the second downed pilot, Fetch53 messaged, "Busy bee," the A4s call sign via radio communication, asking him to release his smoke as he approached. That would help Dave know which way the harness would blow in the wind when his crew lowered it. The downed pilot was unable to release the smoke, so for the second time the delicate maneuver of lowering the hoist until the harness barely kissed the water, and then dragging it to the pilot at a slow speed so it didn't hurt the pilot and he could grab it and put it under his arms, had to be executed.

Once the A4 pilot was safely secured in the harness, Dave moved out as quickly as possible. No need to sit in a hover so anti-aircraft rockets could get a good sighting on his chopper. A moving target is harder to hit. This pilot was not hurt badly and understood the need to search the water for the navigator, despite the risk of being shot down. After a long period of searching, however, they were running low on fuel. Fetch 53 informed the Ranger, his carrier, that the rescued pilots were in stable condition, having received first aid from his crewmen. Fetch 53 was cleared to refuel from Red Crow, a rescue destroyer with refueling capability, and resume the search.

When I read that Dave decided to resume the search in that heavily fortified cauldron of potential death, I caught my breath. A tear clouded my eyes, and I had to remind myself that he was home, and that he was safe. After refueling, they resumed the search to no avail. The navigator from the A6 Intruder, Lt. Marik, must have been badly injured and unable to jettison his parachute. With a heavy heart at the loss of the navigator, Dave flew back to the carrier. This took place the last day of Dave's deployment on the Carrier Ranger for search and rescue duty. After being debriefed and receiving some "atta boys" from the captain, Dave departed the Ranger and rejoined his squadron on the Carrier Yorktown. When I read about this rescue operation after-the-fact, my first thoughts were thankfulness and gratitude that God had protected Dave. His faithfulness overwhelmed me. That rescue was described as one of the most successful rescue operations of the Vietnam war. If only the navigator had survived and been rescued as well, Dave would truly be able to celebrate the day.

As a Navy pilot assigned to Search and Rescue duty stationed on board two different super carriers, the Enterprise and the Ranger, Dave was in harm's way every time he took off because it was the peak of the air war. One day Dave's detachment and the Air Group developed a plan to attempt the rescue of a pilot whose plane had been shot down by a missile 20 miles north of Hanoi and was attempting to evade capture by hiding in the jungle. Two helicopters would fly toward North Vietnam. One would fly in under heavy enemy fire and rescue the downed pilot. The other helicopter was to wait off shore and be ready to rescue the first crew in case they were shot down. Dave said to me, "We were ready to go, but the captain of the Ranger called off the rescue attempt. He thought it was too risky. You know — this was good training for living the Christian life under the authority of our Captain who is God Almighty. If we follow his orders, as revealed to us by the Holy Spirit and the words of the Bible, we will be in the right place and do the right thing." David had the opportunity to save the lives of seven pilots while serving in the Navy.

I thought back to the day in Pensacola, Florida, when Dave told me he wanted to fly jets, if the eye doctor cleared him. That day I listened to fear, which had accosted me immediately, instead of turning to God. If I had said, "Let's pray about that decision," instead of trying to influence the path Dave was to take, I might have heard the Holy Spirit whisper to me, "Lean not on your own understanding, but in all your ways acknowledge Him and He will direct your path" (Proverbs 3:5, 6). But I had not turned to my Heavenly Father and sought the guidance of the Holy Spirit. I reacted by wanting to forge a safe path for Dave myself. I believe that Dave, who understood my fear of losing him and not wanting to have our daughters grow up with the pain of having lost their dad, as I had, was influenced by my fear. In reality, flying low and slow with bullets and rockets being shot at him, in that new jet helicopter was far less safe than Dave would have been in many other types of airplanes. When the Yorktown had completed its mission and was heading back to the States, because I was in the hospital, Dave received permission to fly home instead of riding his Carrier back across the Pacific Ocean.

On the 4th of July in 1966 Dave walked into my hospital room. Tears of joy overflowed from my eyes as we embraced. HE WAS HOME! The joy, elation, and relief I felt was profound. My love, my husband, my children's father, my mother-in-law's son was home safe and sound. Handel's Hallelujah Chorus seemed to be playing loudly inside my mind. "Hallelujah! Hallelujah! Halle- e- lu- u-jah!"

Dave's mother, who had been our rescuer and hero, was happy to return home to the ranch. A couple of days later I was permitted to go home and continue bedrest. Our baby's due date was August 10, just a month away. At home, Dave took very good care of Kristina and me, and our second daughter, Anastasia, was born safely on the first day of August, just ten days earlier than her due date. The first of August was Dave's father's birthday. He often referred to her as his birthday present. He told us that he had a premonition that she would be born on his birthday. We named her Anastasia Mona after my mother and Dave's sister.

When Anastasia was four months old, Dave's parents came to California to meet her and to be present for the award ceremony at the Naval air station. I sat beside them in the front row, with Dave's squadron standing at attention to our left. The admiral of the carrier group, the captain of the carrier, and the commander of the squadron presented Dave with the Distinguished Flying Cross for the heroic rescue of two downed pilots under heavy fire. As I sat there, I recalled some of the words of the Ninety-first Psalm: I had prayed for him throughout his deployment. "Dave dwells in the shelter of the Most High (by faith) and will rest in the shadow of the Almighty. Dave will say to the Lord, "He is my refuge and my fortress, my God in whom I trust." Dave will not fear the terror of night, nor the arrow that flies by day (nor bullets or rockets that fly by day or night)," I had prayed. My heart soared with gratitude as I thanked my Heavenly Father for protecting my husband and for bringing him safely home to me, despite having to be involved in that War. The Bible had taught me a great deal about overcoming fear. "Perfect love casts out fear," (1 John 4:18). That's the love of God. The closer I draw to God, the bigger His love seems to grow and the less I fear anything except losing my relationship with Him.

Chapter Nineteen: *"I AM HE WHOM THOU SEEKEST"*
From the poem "Hound of Heaven" by Francis Thompson

When Dave was not flying or working with the men of the aircraft maintenance division, of which Dave was the commanding officer, he was available to volunteer and be the chaplain. One day, after he had officiated at the Sunday Service, one of his men addressed him. "Sir, have you thought of entering the ministry? I think you would be a really good pastor." Dave told me he had laughed and responded, "I don't know if God can take an engineer and turn him into a theologian!"

Deep within his heart, however, he had felt the calling, even as he argued within himself. After five years of service in the Navy, he submitted his resignation to accept the call of God. In 1967 the Vietnam War was still going hot and heavy and the Navy was in need of pilots. Therefore, the Navy didn't accept his resignation and extended Dave's service obligation for one more year. He received orders to report to the Navy base in Key West, Florida. The long drive from the West Coast to the East Coast provided us with an opportunity to visit a couple of seminaries.

As Dave looked over the curriculum of seminary studies, it confirmed his doubts that without having studied liberal arts courses and courses in ancient history, he would be ill-prepared for seminary. His degree in mathematics and engineering, was not going to be helpful. Unfortunately, at that time some people had entered seminary in order to avoid being drafted by the military. In Cambridge, Massachusetts Dave encountered a group of seminarians dancing around a mummy held up by helium-filled balloons. As it ascended, they chanted "go, go Jesus". Dave couldn't handle the disdain they expressed for his Navy uniform, but the disrespect of the name of Jesus the Christ was shocking and unacceptable. Had they never heard that beautiful hymn "At the name of Jesus every knee shall bow, every tongue confess Him King of glory now?" "There's got to be another way that I can prepare to serve God and reach young people" he told me." "The students I met were more interested in accumulating knowledge, and I don't mean Biblical knowledge; they certainly aren't seeking a personal relationship with Jesus and developing a prayer life," he said as we continued our drive to Key West. He decided not to seek Ordination.

Key West is an Island that is four miles long and one mile wide, and it lies at the southernmost end of US Route 1. After driving from California on the West Coast to the East Coast of the US, visiting family and seminaries along the way, we finally arrived at the southernmost point in America. We reported to the base housing office and discovered there were two options for housing available to us on the Navy base. One was a three-bedroom recently constructed home that looked very nice and modern. The other was a two-bedroom cinderblock bungalow right on the Bay with a boat dock in the backyard. We chose the cinderblock bungalow. The modern conveniences of the newer house could not compete with the view of the water out back of the bungalow. We hung swings for the girls from the mature trees that shaded the backyard. I thought I had arrived in paradise. The ocean breeze wafted away the sun's heat, and the air smelled sweet and fresh. Dave worked reasonable hours — he was home in the morning and in the evening, and the girls were overjoyed to have their Daddy home every day. Dave and I became involved at St. Paul's Church, together teaching junior high Sunday School students. After a few months the minister made a house call. It was a pleasant visit, until he asked Dave if he had considered going into the ministry. "Yes I had, but not anymore," said Dave. "I just don't see how God could turn me into a theologian. I'm an engineer and mathematician. I do see that I am effective working with the young men in my command, and now that I am instructing pilots to fly the Sikorsky helicopter, I am learning that I can keep their attention if I share stories. But that's a lot different than preaching. I haven't studied any ancient history, philosophy or theology. I covet your prayers for what God would have me do next when I leave the Navy."

After the wonderful year in Key West, boating, fishing, and enjoying the semi-tropical climate, we returned to Colorado in late May, Dave having resigned from the Navy. His parents had sold the ranch and built a retirement home on a golf course in Monument, Colorado. During the move, Mykie took a bad fall and broke her hip. They needed help and we were available to provide the help while she healed. We moved into what they called the "annex", a wing of the new home they built to accommodate their children and grandchildren. All our household goods were stored in their basement.

The first morning after we moved in, Mykie came home from the hospital, and Dave's Dad wanted to help me in the kitchen as I prepared breakfast. After putting water in a saucepan and placing it on the burner, he turned around and asked me, "Is the water boiling now?" I looked in the pan of water; a few bubbles had formed on the bottom, but none rose to the surface. I said, "Dad, you have been spoiled, no the water is not yet boiling." We both laughed, and I took over the chore of soft boiling some eggs for them.

Dave had applied for graduate school at the University of Denver, for a course that would prepare him to find a career in University Administration. We had the whole summer to spend with Dave's parents. By fall, when classes were to start and we needed to move, Mykie had recovered well enough to manage without us.

At the University of Denver, we were assigned a two-bedroom apartment in a men's dormitory on the campus. Dave was required to be a counselor, or proctor, of a freshman men's dormitory. We received meal passes for all four of us to eat lunch and dinner in the cafeteria with the students if we wanted; our apartment had a small kitchen. Our daughters, ages two and five, were treated like little sisters by some of the college boys. They carried them on their shoulders and played with them as we walked to and fro from the dining hall.

Dave greeted every student moving into the dorm and tried to meet their parents as well. Some moved in without the company of their parents, but there was one young man whose parents stayed with their student all day. They unpacked for him and promised to come back once a week to pick up his dirty laundry. He had a hard time adjusting to university life.

Dave posted an announcement on the bulletin board that there would be a Bible study in our living room at 10 P.M. Sunday evenings for any of the young men in our dorm who would like to participate. "You're on the staff of the University and you've posted a Bible study. I'm Jewish, and I feel left out," one of the freshmen students challenged Dave. "We will be studying Jeremiah, an Old Testament prophet to learn about his character and how he remained faithful to God through the challenges he faced. I'd like you to come," Dave responded, having made a quick adjustment in what he planned to read and discuss with his students! That young man turned out to be the most faithful participant in the Bible study. I don't think he missed one Sunday evening of the first quarter of school.

A turning point in our lives happened soon after we had settled into university life. Dave's sister-in-law, Diana, went into labor prematurely. Their baby was not due until December but she was born on September 30, 1968, weighing only two pounds and eleven ounces. The next day the baby girl's weight had dropped down to one pound and nine ounces, and she had developed the Hyaline membrane disease. As it happened, that very day, the day after the premature birth, Dave's mother and I had accepted an invitation to attending a luncheon in honor of Dean Pattison, a Canadian Priest. He was in Denver at the invitation of the College of the Rockies and staying with our friends, the Throckmorton's. After introductions and greetings our conversation turned to the deep concern Mykie and I felt for the wee baby. Could she survive, and even if she did, what disabilities could there be; after all she had been blue from oxygen deprivation? We remembered that a few years back President and Mrs. Kennedy had lost a baby who weighed five pounds at birth and then developed Hyaline membrane disease. The prospect for our baby, who only weighed 1 lb. 9 oz. when she developed the Highland membrane disease, was dire. This became the center of our conversation. Father Pattison shared stories of miraculous healings he had seen God preform in many parts of the world. He prayed for our baby, and then he asked if he could pray for me. I was surprised. *I'm fine*, I thought, *I don't need prayer, the baby needs prayer.* I changed the subject as if I had not heard his question. He asked again if he could pray for me, and he encouraged me to ask the Holy Spirit to come and pray through me and guide me in my prayers. "God is the same yesterday today and forever," he said. I felt awkward, yet how could I say no to a priest who wanted to pray for me? Reluctantly, I agreed. As he began to pray, I turned my attention to God. I didn't listen to Dean Pattison's prayer; I was silently pleading for my Heavenly Father to protect me from anything that was not His Will and help me to be available and open to all He had for me. By the end of our prayer and at the end of the luncheon I was so inspired and impressed that upon returning home I encouraged Dave to attend the evening lecture Dean Pattison was delivering, as guest speaker, at the College of the Rockies. After Dave departed, I couldn't wait for the girls to go to sleep so that, with our home quiet, I could spend some time praying for our one-pound baby niece.

I was on my knees by our bed when I heard the front door open. Surprised, I looked at the clock. How could one hour have passed so quickly? In prayer, I had never experienced such deep communion with my heavenly Father before that evening. I felt joyful and expectant and I wanted to continue to thank God for all of his love. That afternoon I had gained a better understanding of the Trinity: One God, one Almighty God who reveals himself to us as Father, Son, and Holy Spirit, equal and indivisible, immutable (which means unchanging). I became more expectant that the Holy Spirit would speak to me when I prayed, meditated, and when I read the Bible.

Dave too was more open to the guidance of the Holy Spirit consequently, his doubts that God could transform an engineer into a theologian were vanquished and he at last said "yes" to God's call and applied for admission to seminary. **The Hound of Heaven had used Dr. Pattison to reveal to Dave that he did not have to depend on his own skills and wisdom, but instead he could trust that the Holy Spirit would empower him to do what God was asking of him.**

Believing that God is a God of order and therefore he should not abandon the course of study he had begun, Dave requested and received permission from the University of Denver to complete the two-year Master's degree program in twelve months. When permission was granted to double up on classes and complete the degree in 12 months Dave perceived that God truly was calling him and opening doors.

Christ Church, the church we were attending, enthusiastically approved and supported his decision. Dave had to go before the Standing Committee of the Diocese to be questioned and receive their approval and then pass a psychiatric evaluation. He had to be interviewed by Bishop Thayer, who after a lengthy conversation recognized Dave's decision as a call from God and gave his approval. Lastly, Dave had to decide on which seminary to apply to. After visiting several seminaries, he decided to apply to Nashotah House in Wisconsin, because when he visited that Seminary, he saw a worshiping community.

The summer before departing for seminary we spent as many weekends as possible with Dave's parents at their golf club community near Colorado Springs. Since Dave's dad and Anastasia shared a birthday on the first of August, it was going to be a multigenerational celebration. Before the evening festivities Dad asked to take Anastasia shopping for her birthday present — her first pair of cowboy boots. He told the saleslady it was their birthday. The sales lady said to Anastasia, "How nice! You were born on the same day as your Pop Pop." Anastasia, age three, looked thoughtfully for a moment, and then said, "Yes, but not the same year." "I am glad you clarified that," said Dad laughing. The sales lady and I chuckled as well. I always enjoyed hearing what my little, precocious daughter had to say.

At the end of the summer, after Dave had received his Master's Degree we packed up for the move to Wisconsin. It was sad for the girls to leave their grandparents and relocate miles away to Wisconsin.

Chapter Twenty: *A NEW CAREER AND GROWING IN FAITH*

"Rise, clasp My hand, and come,"
from THE HOUND OF HEAVEN by Francis Thompson.

Nashotah House Seminary is located on the shores of a small lake about an hour's drive from Milwaukee, Wisconsin. Most of our belongings were still stored in Dave's parents' basement. The few things we were bringing with us were packed in a trailer hitched to our Ford Station Wagon. After two days of driving, we pulled up to the married student quarters, called The Flats, on the vast, park like, property of Nashotah House Seminary. Kristina was the first one to jump out of the car and run into our assigned unit. While I gathered my purse and readied myself to get out of the car, she was already coming back and getting into the car. "I'm not living there," she said as she sat down in the back seat. "Let's go in and see; I'm sure you couldn't have seen all of it," I said. "Yes, I did. I'm not living there," she insisted. I went in and assessed the situation. Yes indeed, she had seen all there was to see in one quick glance. The living room was about twelve feet long by ten feet wide, with a couch against one wall and two doors on the opposite wall leading to the bedrooms. One of the bedrooms was about the size of a king size bed. The kitchen floor space was two by three feet. When Dave and Anastasia came in Kristina followed. "See, I told you," she said. "We'll make it work. We'll move the bunk bed to the larger room so you'll have a play area. The queen bed and one dresser should fit in the other, and once we bring our things in it will begin to feel 'more homey,'" I tried to reassure her and myself. Dave, who had visited the campus, chimed in. "Wait until you see the lake and the beautiful campus. There is a farm as well. I think you will end up enjoying it," he said brightly. He was so right. Three years later, when Dave graduated, the girls did not want to leave Nashotah House, the beautiful campus and our wee little flat.

Our three years at seminary, in Wisconsin, were challenging and rewarding. They flew by quickly. Weekdays always started with worship in the chapel for all the seminarians, then academic work in classrooms and ministry in one of the local churches on the weekends. The children and I attended whichever church Dave was assigned to serve. During the summer his training continued at a Milwaukee hospital. It was important preparation for counseling people facing a health crisis.

I had been involved with Bible studies, for six years before Dave accepted the call to full-time ministry. Therefore, at seminary I took advantage of the opportunity to audit a few classes.

Ever since my encounter with Christ, I had talked to God and now I was learning terms like intercession, petition, thanksgiving, adoration and meditation. I learned that when I prayed for Dave's safety, or for my sister, when she had appendix surgery shortly after we escaped from the Nazis, I was praying an intercessory prayer. When I prayed about my lost trunk, or for God to relieve me of my fear, I was offering a prayer of petition. **When I was a child and felt very lonely, I used to think about God and the love of Jesus by reliving the experience of my vision, and abiding in His Love, loving Him and thanking Him, I learned that was called adoration and meditation.** The prayer of thanksgiving was something I tended to ceaselessly lift up, just out of habit, because I had so much to be grateful for.

During Dave's third year of study, Father Barnes, the Rector of Christ Church, in Denver, Colorado offered him a job upon his graduation. He would serve as the curate, an assistant pastor to the rector, the head pastor. Christ Church was the church we attended during the 12 months Dave studied at the University of Denver. Dave and I had been praying that God would prepare us for wherever we could best serve the Lord. We were delighted to learn we would be returning to Denver and faced the last semester with calm assurance of where the next move would take our family.

With excitement we invited both sides of our family to be with us in Denver for Dave's Ordination service. Aunt Doris, Dave's saintly Godmother and Dad's older sister, still lived in St. Andrews, Scotland, so she was unable to attend. As an Ordination present, she sent a generous gift — the down payment to purchase a house, the first home we owned. We felt settled and with enthusiasm entered the work of the church.

The first day of work, after Dave's ordination, he was asked to visit a parishioner in the hospital. Upon arriving he discovered a very sad scene. The surgeon had reported to the family that he discovered Isabel's cancer was so advanced and widespread that he had closed up the abdomen knowing that he was unable to remove all the cancer. After some of the teary-eyed people had left her room, and only the immediate family remained, Dave explained that he had come to anoint her for healing with Holy Oil and offer her Communion. With the fervor of the newly ordained priest, Dave said, "the Bible tells us to pray for the sick and they shall recover; I believe God can heal you". Batting her eyes, with a little smile on her face Isabel, a very Godly women, responded "I too believe He can heal me." And so, it happened. Isabel lived for at least ten more productive years. During those ten years her husband, who had never darkened the threshold of a church before, accepted Jesus as his Lord and Savior and was baptized. When she died the autopsy revealed that there was no cancer anywhere in her abdomen.

A few weeks after Dave had started this new ministry, he complained to me that there was nothing going on at church during the week. "I'd like to start a Bible study in our home Wednesday nights if Father Barnes agrees, what do you think?"

I thought that was a fabulous idea, I could participate and we wouldn't need a babysitter. In the fall the Bible Study was announced at all the services and our address was printed in the bulletin. We were both excited the first evening of the scheduled study as seven o'clock drew near. Who would come? Would anyone come, we wondered? No sooner had our ships bell clock sounded the hour when our door bell began to ring. Soon our small living room was overcrowded and Dave suggested we move down to the playroom in the lower level.

About thirty-five parishioners arrived for that first study. After Dave opened with prayer, he presented a short exposition on the first 14 verses of John's Gospel, and then asked for comments or questions. A young lady's hand shot up exclaiming, "I have a friend who is the happiest person I know; she is just aglow all the time. She told me that was because she was a born-again Christian. I want what she has but I don't know how?"

Dave said, "What a great question, let's skip ahead to Chapter three in John's Gospel. Would someone like to read verses one through sixteen for us?"

Everyone listened intently as these powerful verses were read with Jesus telling Nicodemus that he must be born again. Then Dave referred to verse five following and read, "I tell the truth, no one can enter the Kingdom of God unless he is born of water and the Spirit. Flesh gives birth to flesh, but Spirit gives birth to spirit. You should not be surprised at my saying, You must be born again. The wind blows where it pleases. You hear its sound, but you cannot tell where it comes from or where it is going, so it is with everyone born of the Spirit." Then Dave asked her, "Is this what you are seeking, would you like to be born anew?" "Yes, yes with all my heart," she said.

Then Dave led her in a sinner's prayer and invited all present to pray for the Holy Spirit to live in her heart, so she would know with certainty that Jesus Christ is her Lord and Savior. This surprising move of the Holy Spirit was the spark that ignited the renewal that began in Christ Church in 1972.

A year and a half after we had settled into our new home near Christ Church and the girls had started school, Father Barnes announced his retirement. You can imagine our surprise and disappointment. He had discovered that he had a large brain tumor, which was causing him to be exceedingly tired. At a meeting of the vestry (the lay leaders of the parish), Father Barnes announced his decision. The Rector of an Episcopal Church chooses his assistants. For us, this meant that we would, most likely, need to sell our home and move again.

David and I had been meeting at the church several days a week to kneel at the Altar rail and pray for renewal. We prayed that the dear people in this congregation would experience the love of God and the joy of a personal, intimate relationship with Jesus. We prayed that the Holy Spirit would come and enliven our faith and lead us into all truth of God's Word as we studied the Bible together. One day as we prayed, I had what I can only describe as a vision of Dave officiating at the Altar of the church. I could see that the congregation had experienced renewal, because every seat was taken and people were actively engaged in worship. At the time I did not tell Dave about the vision, except to say that I believed revival was coming.

It was logical, at least in my mind, that the vision was of a time far in the future. I thought that Dave, after a three-year period of training under Father Barnes, would then become head pastor of a small church in the mountains. After several years he then could be called back to Christ Church, a congregation we had grown to love. That was logical, but a move so soon? The girls were just beginning to feel settled in their new school. That's what I was thinking about when Dave came home earlier than expected one day and said, "Katrina, come sit down. You won't believe this! Richard Massey, the senior warden, came in my office today to talk to me and tell me that the vestry feels the best decision they could make would be to have me continue at the Church and become the next Rector. I explained to him that that was against diocesan policy, but he insisted that the majority of the vestry was of one mind. They felt the church was coming alive, and they did not want to quench the Spirit with a change of leadership."

I didn't know how to respond, we sat in silence for a few moments, unsettled, yet seeking the inner voice of the Holy Spirit. Then I remembered the vision I had while we had prayed for the church. I described the picture I had in my mind of the vision to Dave and asked, "What do you think about that? Christ Church full, with the people engaged in active worship?" "There is no way.

There are many very good clergy with more experience they could choose from, and it's against diocesan policy," Dave responded, looking thoughtful. "Remember that day, when after we had prayed, I said that I believe revival was coming to Christ Church? Could it be that God gave me that vision because he wants to do something unusual?"

We sat silently, lost in the conflicting thoughts, each looking down at the floor, seeking the Lord, seeking His peace. Then Dave suggested that we pray together for God's Will to be done. Afterwards, Dave decided not to decline the invitation from the vestry and to leave it up to God and the Bishop. He said, "If the vestry is unanimous and the Bishop approves me for that position, which would be out of the ordinary, I think it would confirm it is a call from God."

The senior warden informed us that the vestry was going down to speak with the Bishop, and convince him that Dave was the right man for the job. The Bishop requested that they go through a search process and interview six clergy whom he recommended. If after a thorough discernment process, they still believed young Father Dave Wilson was the right man for the job, he would allow it.

When Dave told me about that, he repeated what he had said earlier, "There are so many great and more experienced clergy for them to choose from. Could this really be God's Will?" With a smile I said, recalling several verses from different parts of the Bible, "God chooses the foolish to confound the wise. God chooses whom He will. When we are weak, then He is strong."

After a few months of the uncertainty, while the search committee interviewed the six people recommended by the Bishop and prayerfully sought the guidance of the Holy Spirit, the vestry asked Dave to come before them. As the assistant he had continued his work but had not heard any whispers of what the search committee and vestry were talking about.

Dave had been gone for about an hour, and the girls were settled in their beds and asleep when the doorbell rang. I opened the door to see Mr. and Mrs. Whiting. Mr. Whiting asked me if I would come with him to the church and said that his wife would stay with the children. I looked at them with such a surprise while wondering "do they want to interview me as well?" Then Mr.

Whiting got the biggest grin on his face and said, "Don't worry." I surmised from his smile and the sparkle in his eyes that we would not be uprooting our family again with another move. They had talked and prayed and eventually Dave had accepted the unanimous call to be Rector of Christ Church. I was invited to be part of their little celebration.

The next day on my way to Bible Study I ran into Father Barnes, who with a big grin on his face expressed his delight at the Vestry's decision, giving me a big hug. The job of Rector at Christ Church kept Dave busy twenty hours a day, seven days a week; but he loved it and he realized that he had found his purpose in life.

On his first Christmas Eve as Rector he arrived home after three services, sometime around 1:30 in the morning, having been on his feet most of the day. Yet there was no rest for the weary. At home there were toys waiting to be assembled for the girls. I had already filled the stockings, and was waiting for him with some hot toddies and all the toys that needed to be assembled in time for "Santa" to arrive. In a very tired voice, he said, "Boy, they sure didn't tell us about this in seminary." It seemed like we had just laid our heads on the pillow when the girls raced into our bedroom giggling with much excitement to celebrate Christmas morning together.

While David was in seminary, I had the opportunity to audit several classes and plumb the depths of wisdom of the Word of God as recorded in the Bible. As a member of Christ Church, I wanted to continue to study the Scriptures with the ladies in our church. I was thirsty for more and more of His revelation of Himself and invited the women of our Church to join me. We studied and meditated together, forging wonderful friendships, prayer partners, and supports groups. I recognized my need for His wisdom, and so did my new friends. We saw the importance and the impact of His Word as Dave taught and preached it in our congregation. Renewal and growth were evident. One of the fruits of growth was the ability to support missionaries to Africa and many needs in the community.

The Saint Francis Center was one cause that we started as a joint venture with the Diocese of Colorado. It provided a place for homeless people to have a shower, do their laundry, and receive a sandwich for lunch. Many of the ladies who volunteered at the St.

Francis Center from our church were of retirement age. They came to my husband with a problem that looking back on it makes me giggle. Since these men had been living on the street for years, they had forgotten about basic manners for obvious reasons. While using the center's laundry room, some of them would put all their clothes in the washing machine and then walk around stark naked until their clothes were dry. The look of surprise on the elderly women's faces was priceless, and their eyes were as big as saucers while looking anywhere but towards the naked men helping themselves to coffee. After a few chuckles, Dave suggested we have a "boxers and briefs" Sunday. If every parishioner brought one pair to donate when they came to worship, the Center would have plenty to give to each man when they arrived to wash their clothes and shower. It was very successful, and our volunteer ladies were relieved that no one would be walking around buck naked. This center also provided sandwiches and secure mailboxes, so that people living on the streets had an address to give if they applied for a job, for housing, or some other need.

Growth in church membership also meant that there was a need for more programs. One day David asked me if I would give a talk, including my testimony, at the fall luncheon to kick off women's ministry programs. I said I would pray about it. I didn't like to think about that painful time of leaving my home in Latvia and losing my father. The thought of talking about it was unnerving. As I prayed, I was reminded of the day I met Jim Wilson. **"What God had whispered to me in the dark, in the Baltic Sea, I needed to speak of in the light of day."**

I had given a couple of talks while Dave was still in the Navy. His commanding officer's wife had asked if I would speak at an officers' wives' luncheon, which I did. I presented a historical perspective. I had spoken about my family's ancient roots in Latvia, dating back to the sixteenth century and Latvia's ancient history dating back to before the Bronze Age. I spoke about World War II and the evolution of two strains of Marxism: Marxism as Lenin interpreted it in Russia, and the brutality Stalin employed to institute it, and Marxism as the root of Fascism, as Hitler instituted it overthrowing the fledgling democracy in Germany.

That always surprised the audience, as American schools simplistically teach that Communism is left wing and Fascism is right wing and that they are opposites to each other. Marx, however, while studying at the University of Berlin, had developed a following in Germany. Later Hitler became a spokesman for a group of German Communists who wanted to overthrow the government as the Communists had done in Russia under Lenin's leadership. Some in the German Communist Party were in close contact with Communists and Russians. That was unacceptable to Hitler, therefore, he called his party the National Socialist Party. He wanted to be totally independent and not in any way associated with Stalin in Russia. Stalin's and Hitler's ideological ambitions for a one world government had set them against each other and eventually that set the world on fire. It was still the source of a piercing pain in my heart, so therefore, I never shared very much of my personal experience.

Now Dave was asking me to speak and share my personal experiences in the War and my encounter with Jesus. That was much more difficult for me and I felt very vulnerable the first time I shared my testimony. It was a lovely luncheon and as I spoke, I saw that I had the full attention of all the ladies. Several had tears in their eyes at times. I held my tears back until I finished my testimony, and then I went into the Church and knelt at the Altar rail and had a good cry. David came in and prayed for me, and our dear Lord's healing touch strengthened me. As hard as that first time speaking about my personal experience was, it must have brought fruit for God's Kingdom. After that first talk, I received many invitations to speak. Quite frequently at the conclusion of my testimony women would come up to me and ask if I was going to have a book signing. "Oh no, I'm a storyteller I'm certainly not an author," I would respond. God has a sense of humor, doesn't he?

One evening, after I had spoken to a gathering in a Presbyterian Church, the pastor asked me "do you really believe that it was Jesus himself you saw that night you were escaping?" He seemed to be concerned about that part of my testimony. "When I was six-years-old, I was convinced that Jesus had come to rescue me, and I think He did, but does it matter? Does it matter if it was Jesus or a messenger, an Angel, who reflected Jesus, reflected the pure all-knowing Love of God so bright that from that time forward I never feared death or doubted the existence of God?" I asked. He nodded his head thoughtfully. I continued, **"God wants everyone**

to know He is near and He loves you dearly, that's the important thing I saw, I learned."

"All things work together for good to those who are called according to God's purpose," (Romans 8:28). In the economy of our heavenly Father, the bad things, the tragedies, and heartaches of our life, are not wasted. All the times I shared my testimony I never spoke about having been sexually abused, not once. I discovered, however, that in ministry God could use me to help other victims of sexual abuse in the parish. One day Dave called me at home and asked, "Would you be free around one o'clock tomorrow to come to my office?" "I think so, let me doublecheck. Why, what's up?" I inquired as I went to look at my calendar. "Do you remember meeting Mary Jones? She comes to church by herself. I had an appointment with her today, and she told me that her husband had agreed to come and talk with me if you were present. Years ago, when he was a member of the boys' choir in his church the choirmaster had singled him out and complimented him about his great voice. To prepare for his solos he had to spend time with him alone, after a while he had started to sexually abuse him. Once he had the courage to free himself from the abuse, and the threats that followed, he has never darkened the door of a church again. She was so hopeful that we could help him; she said that it is a big step that he has agreed to come to my office if my wife is present." "Wow, that's a biggie," I said. "Of course, I will be there. I'll start praying for that appointment today. May our Lord's healing touch set him free."

The next day as Dave and I greeted the Joneses and listened to him recall his experience of abuse in the church, we prayed, we shared and evangelized and listened prayerfully. Dave counseled, and then we prayed silently as we watched him cry — tears that needed to be shed from so long ago. Leaning over, with his elbows on his knees, his face in his hands and his shoulders shaking, he cried. Then we saw God's healing touch restore the innocence of the child within this fifty-year-old man. I, still in my thirties, felt young and entirely inadequate. God, in his love knew how to reach and heal Steve Jones. Since the choirmaster had been an older man, Dave, a young priest, and I, having experienced sexual abuse myself, were the right people, through whom God could administer His healing grace.

A few years earlier I had experienced inner healing at a retreat. Our retreat leader was a wonderful speaker and author who reflected the love of God brightly. In one of the meditations, she talked about someone who needed to forgive a parent for dying. I thought that was a disrespectful statement, why would one need to forgive a parent who suffered an untimely death? I went to speak with her after she had concluded her presentation. She asked me, "Did you experience a parent dying when you were a child?" "Yes, I did. I love and respect my dad, and he died because he fought and worked for the freedom of Latvia and against the oppression of Stalin and Hitler; that's why I don't understand forgiving a loving parent or a sovereign God." She said, "Have you ever had any fears of abandonment?" I had to think back, and after a moment I said, "Well maybe, when my mother was very ill and my Papa was dead, and then, I guess when Dave wanted to be a pilot my fear of him flying jets was probably rooted in fear of abandonment?" She responded, "That is very common; I have prayed with a lot of people whose parents died when they were a child. They were set free of fear and then began to trust the relationships they were in as a result of forgiving God and their parent who had died. I helped them believe what Jesus said, 'I will be with you always.' He will give you His peace and set you free." "May I pray with you?," she asked.

As the years went by, our family life and church life were intricately woven together. Our daughters were active in the youth group, singing in the choir, and Anastasia volunteered as a reader of Scripture and acolyte for the Sunday morning worship services. Kristina was involved with Young Life at her school as well as the youth group and choir at the church. She frequently invited the whole Young Life group to come to our house for home-baked pizza, which she made from scratch. When she was a rising senior in high school, she volunteered to go on a mission trip to Haiti. The letters we received during her two weeks of training in Florida were joyful and inspiring.

After she arrived in Haiti, however, her letters started to concern us. The adult leadership of that particular group did not seem to be following the protocol of the organization sponsoring that mission trip. The young people who had raised money to build a schoolhouse for an orphanage, located in a remote area of Haiti, were enthusiastic and compassionate for the children they met. It was easy for their leadership to manipulate them and make them feel guilty for wanting to take a break from work in the middle of the day, which they were supposed to do. The midday temperature rose above one hundred and ten degrees, yet they would continue to work, carrying bags of cement and other heavy labor. On the weekends, instead of taking them to the beach, the adults encouraged them to swim in the canal. Daily they were told to bathe in the dirty water of the canal, where native neighbors upstream allowed all body waste to flow. Kristina and several other children became deathly ill.

Some tropical parasites that entered her bloodstream were not diagnosed for three years. They were unknown and unseen by American doctors in Colorado. By the time they were diagnosed, with the help of a hospital in Miami, Florida, they had caused damage to her kidneys, her liver, and even entered her spinal column. As a family and a church community we had prayed for discernment and healing. My heart ached in seeing my child suffer. I often thought about Mother Mary, standing beneath the cross. How brave she must have been, how strong — the Saintly Lady, Mother of our Lord Jesus Christ.

What I was going through, watching my daughter's deteriorating health, was not nearly as heart breaking. Nevertheless, it hurt all of us. Kristina dwindled down to eighty-nine pounds of skin and bones before the correct diagnosis was given. During that painful time, I was so grateful for our Church, which had become like a real family. I needed the ladies of my Bible Study to minister to me. Sometimes I was angry with God. I had seen miraculous healings. *Why not my child?* I became so intent on finding a cure for her, she became my number one focus. In retrospect I recognize I was not seeking the Lord with my whole heart at that time. My focus was on getting the answer to what I wanted. My focus was on the illness rather than on the Healer. What a blessing to be a part of a Christian community in a time of crisis! I needed their wisdom and support. I needed their prayer support.

Anastasia continued with her schooling, sports, and singing during this trying time. However, when Anastasia was invited to represent her school on a trip to Europe, which was quite an honor, we became concerned. Who would she be traveling with, what family would she be staying with, etc. I spoke with my mother about my concerns, hoping she would alleviate them. Instead, she concurred with Dave and me. She said; "You let one daughter go off with strangers and she came home very sick, are you going to let your other daughter travel with strangers?"

Well, that was that, we said "NO!" The trip to Europe for academic achievement would have been much safer and very different from working in unsanitary conditions in Haiti, the poorest country in the Western Hemisphere. I hope Anastasia has forgiven us. We wanted Anastasia to be free of the worry we carried and enjoy her high school years, but there was no way to shield her from the dark shadow of concern that hovered over our family.

Even when I attended her lacrosse games and concerts and was truly happy seeing Anastasia having a good time, at the back of my mind was the weight of concern. She was lead singer in a little band, which on occasion was invited to play for junior high school dances. The year her school put on "The King and I" as their annual Musical, Anastasia was thrilled to be chosen to play the part of Anna, the lead character. Either Dave or I went to every performance. We were so happy that Dave's parents, Mykie and Pop Pop, were able to drive up one night to see the Musical. I discovered that I could possess the emotions of happiness in the shadow of sadness, experiencing both feelings at the very same time.

With hindsight I know it was a mistake for us to try to protect Anastasia from the reality of life in our family. She saw how much we had to do for her sister. We just did not keep her informed about some of the medical facts of the situation, and I think it made her feel excluded and not a part of what we were going through. I became too focused on trying to be a savior of them both, instead of trusting my Savior with them and our situation.

Kristina soldiered on with her education despite several month-long hospitalizations. Her senior year in high school was anything but normal, but she graduated with honors and went on to university in the fall on an academic scholarship. Before the year was out, however, we received a call from the administration. They said they could not be responsible for a student in such seriously bad health. She returned home and became a day student at the University of Denver. Her studies continued to be interrupted by needed hospitalizations, until at last, the diagnosis of tropical parasites was made. When she finally started to heal and put some weight back on, I felt like a hundred-pound weight had been lifted from my back.

Anastasia was about to graduate from high school and head to Colorado State University. It was a university that had a good Broadcasting Journalism major which she was interested in pursuing. Life was returning to an even keel. Then Dave received an invitation to become the Rector of All Saints Church in Winter Park, Florida. After we prayed together for a couple of days, we decided it was a call of God on our lives and accepted the invitation.

After serving the church in Denver for twelve years, and both of our daughters were out of the nest studying at universities, Dave felt that the Lord was calling him to a new challenge and a new congregation. It was so hard to say goodbye to all our dear friends and Dave's parents in Colorado, and move two thousand miles away, but we knew it was a call from God and, therefore, we trusted that it would be good.

All Saints Church in Winter Park, Florida, was an historic old church with a rich history and well-established congregation. The congregation consisted of mostly mature people. One day soon after our arrival, I asked Dave, "I have been praying for direction, how can I serve the Lord in this parish, do you have any idea?" He suggested that it would be very helpful if I formed a prayer circle to pray for the church. Dave believed every work of God needed to be undergirded by prayer. In his first year at All Saints Church, he was presiding at very many funerals but few baptisms. He said he needed the guidance of the Holy Spirit and asked us to pray for renewal for the congregation. Some of the ladies in the Church joined me and we started to meet in the chapel for one hour concentrating on the Lord and seeking His revelation for the work of the Church. One of the prayer warriors I met was quite elderly, and she had been praying for the Church all by herself for many years. She was delighted to have several young women join her. She was an inspirational saint; I was privileged to learn from her.

This congregation included a plethora of gifted individuals, people who when they heard the Word of God, believed in Jesus as Savior and Lord, and wanted to grow in faith and bless others. Year after year many families with children joined the congregation.

Now Dave presided at many weddings and baptisms. On a Sunday, known as All Saints Sunday, we had eighteen baptisms spread over five worship services. The Holy Spirit was at work.

Some of the students in our congregation heard about my ancestry and invited me to speak at their schools when their class was studying World War II. After one of my talks, a young lady asked, "Did I hear you refer to Hitler as being involved in the German Communist Party? I thought he was a Fascist. Aren't they opposites?" "You are correct that they were opposed to each other," I responded. I continued, "During the brief period of democracy in Germany, after World War I, Hitler was active in the German Communist Party — he was influenced by Marx. Marx had studied at the University of Berlin until he was kicked out because of his radical and militant activity. Subsequently, his writings influenced both Hitler and Stalin. Hitler split from the German Communists because he did not like their connection and loyalty to Communists in Russia. That's why he called his party the National Socialist Party. He accepted help from the Communists in Germany to consolidate his authority over the German people, but a few years after he was granted absolute power, he arrested all the leading German Communists who had connections to the Communist Party in Moscow." The teachers present never disputed or questioned this information which was new to them as well. I was often surprised at the shallow, one-dimensional understanding of history so many students had, when complex ideas are abbreviated it's easy to come to an incorrect conclusion.

Dave and I learned to love the people of All Saints Church deeply and felt such joy in seeing their faith grow, especially when we had the privilege of witnessing conversions. The Church became a loving community. All Saints had a special relationship with a ministry in Honduras, which was our companion diocese. About a year after we arrived in Central Florida, Dave joined a group of parishioners and visited the orphanage for abandoned boys in Tegucigalpa, Honduras, called "The Home of Love and Hope." "The boys love for Jesus blessed my socks off," Dave told me when he returned home.

That group, which included a veterinarian, identified several areas of need that our parish would address. Vocational training for the boys was part of the program, so that they could be self-sufficient when they graduated. Everyone agreed that was paramount because when they would be leaving the school at the age of 18 or 19, they had no family to go to. A technical school for welding and carpentry met that need. The veterinarian identified a problem at the farm, where boys, not skilled in mechanics, were able to learn agriculture. At the farm they were milking brahma cows, who produce very little milk. If we wanted them to have a productive dairy, we needed to send them Jersey or Guernsey milk cows. Dave, having grown up on a ranch, understood the problem and agreed wholeheartedly. He asked the vet, "Would you accompany the yearlings from the US and care for their health for the first year, or so, until they became acclimated to the conditions in Honduras: the different parasites, weather, food, etc?" "Absolutely, I'll commit to do that and I'll return several times the first year to inoculate the calves if the church raised the money to purchase them," he responded. "That's great! Those that survive the first year will become good milk producing cows." The vet having agreed, All Saints parishioners got busy, and in many creative and fun ways they raised the money needed to purchase the yearlings.

We also wanted every graduate from the technical school to receive tools that he would need after graduation to enable him to support himself by working in his learned trade. We prayed that they would grow up to be Godly and self-sufficient men. I mention this particular ministry because of how much I learned from this work; I learned how to develop an effective outreach in another country and the organizational needs that were required, etc. Years later what I learned from this work enabled me to launch Baltic Outreach.

While we were serving in this parish, the stronghold that the Soviet Union held over occupied countries behind the Iron Curtain since WWII was loosened. **Anna and I were able to take Mama back to Latvia for a visit in 1989**. That visit was written about in the Latvian newspaper which Mr. Pancis read. Another article had described my work in bringing the Riga Dome Boys Choir to perform in Central Florida and at Disney World. That's what enabled Mr. Pancis to track me down and call me.

Chapter Twenty-One: *RETURN TO LATVIA – 1989*

"All which thy child's mistake fancies as lost, I have stored for thee at Home"
from THE HOUND OF HEAVEN by Francis Thompson

In the summer of 1989 Mama, Anna, and I joined a group of physicians who had planned a medical conference and educational tour of Latvia. Perestroika, an economic restructuring required because the Communist economic policies had made the ruble worthless, had brought about a loosening of restrictions in the USSR, making travel easier and safer into occupied Latvia. I suspect the Soviet Union needed the viable currency foreign tourists would bring. Perestroika had also loosened restrictions on the people of the Soviet Union who had lived behind the Iron Curtain since 1945, without freedom to travel from East Europe to the free world, as well as making it easier for us to visit Latvia.

A chartered Soviet airplane flew the members of our group from Helsinki, Finland to Riga, Latvia. It was the first flight from the free world in forty-five years to land in Riga without having to fly to Moscow first. We were so excited, and more than a little nervous, as we landed. Clutching my American passport, I stepped from the USSR airplane onto Latvian soil. Fear, born from my escape forty-five years earlier, caused my heart to beat wildly. My impulse was to kneel and kiss the soil of the land of my birth, the land my father loved so well that he was willing to give his life. But beneath my feet was only black asphalt, put there by foreign invaders. Soviet soldiers with weapons in their hands and expressionless faces formed a pathway for us to the door of the terminal building. Anna and I guided our mother towards passport control. Reporters had read on the airplane manifest that Anastasija Čakste was on this flight. They inquired for "that important person," who has arrived, "a Mrs. Čakste."

Soon they surround my eighty-year-old mother with arms outstretched, holding microphones to her face, peppering her with questions. She has her own memories of the events I have described. She knew a great deal of the dangerous work my Papa was involved in — she had played a part in it. My Apapa, her father Antons Stipnieks, had financed the fishermen who smuggled letters to the Latvian Embassy in Sweden, which were then passed on to the Allies. He said after Papa's arrest, "If I had known what Tuntans (my dad's nickname) needed the money for, I would not have given it to him."

Apap had also provided well for our escape. All the buttons on our coats and jackets were cloth covered gold coins given to us by Apap. Mama never saw her parents again, and yet here she was in her fatherland again, something she had not expected in her lifetime. Even with congestive heart failure, she was not going to miss this trip — to once more be in the land she fought and sacrificed for. "How sad to see my beautiful Riga in such a dreadful state of disrepair, still with damage from the war so many years later." That was all she could say, shaking her head. We suggested to the reporters that this interview could take place later, after Mrs. Čakste had a rest from the long flights.

At passport control I felt all my muscles tighten. I took several deep breaths to calm my beating heart. *Communists never forget,* I thought. My husband and daughters had worried about my safety, remembering the stories I had told them. When we were living in Uppsala, Sweden, the Soviet sympathizers who had taken over the Latvian Embassy in Stockholm came to our house more than once to invite us to return to Latvia. They had written letters, the last one suggesting that if we didn't accept their kind invitation to return home, when they occupied Sweden, it would not be so comfortable for us. *Are we still on their blacklist, so many years later?* I wondered.

I handed my passport to the inspector, saying a prayer in my mind as he read, "American citizen born in Riga, Latvia." He looked at me, then without a word stamped my passport and returned it to me. I exhaled as I joined my family and proceeded out the door. We were pleasantly surprised to see kind people greeting us and filling our arms with flowers. Joy rose in me, and I felt emboldened to join marches for freedom alongside these dear people who had suffered serfdom under Communism. Yes, they had free dental care, but I was told that Novocain was not available for most of them when drilling deep cavities. They had free medical care, but the well-educated doctors didn't have the medicines they needed. There was one sonogram machine, but it wasn't available to everyone. The children's hospital had the same cribs and other equipment it had in the 1939 photographs of the children's hospital. Communist government officials could get medication and modern medical care that they needed because they were important. *They need to be healthy for the good of the population* was the excuse of the party. But the population suffered.

So, we marched, my sister and I, along with thousands of other Latvians. Most of the marchers and leaders had not experienced the glory of free Latvia before WWII. They were too young. *Since God created people with a free will*, I thought, *it is natural for these young people to long for freedom, to make their own choices*. Through all those years of occupation, some defied the USSR government and went to my grandfather's grave on days that hadn't been national holidays, to light candles, even though threatened with prison. Jānis Čakste represented the freedom of democracy — the dignity of responsible self-governance that was our heritage. As we marched with Latvian flags waving, we marched toward the "Statue of Liberty" in Riga, a tall statue of "Mother Latvia" reaching her arms to the sky with three stars in her hands. On that day, all of us had hope that someday soon Latvia would once more be free.

In 1989 the street cars in Riga were crowded but the roads were empty - very few people, other than government officials, had cars. When relatives invited us for dinner, we overheard them discussing the chores required of each one. They had to get up early and go to the stores. One was to go stand in the line at the bakery, one to the butcher shop, and another for the vegetables and salad. They had to get up early to get in line before the food sold out. We felt a little embarrassed to be such a burden, so we decided to go to a bakery on our way in the afternoon. In the window I saw loaves of bread, but inside there was nothing left. All the bakeries were empty by the afternoon.

Under the Soviet regime a baker could not change a recipe without getting permission from Moscow - no one could add an extra spoon of vanilla, for example. All bakeries carried the same thing; competition was not allowed. In my youth, Schwartzes Cafe and Bakery had a plethora of choices of tempting pastries. With longing and warm memories, I recalled the aroma when stepping into that little café. At the back of the bakery were small round tables and red velvet chairs, where Mama would meet a friend for a cup of coffee and a visit. Under Communism, sales ladies got paid whether they pleased the customers or not. They hurried us away, saying, "Tomorrow, tomorrow." The Dollar Store, so called because it did not accept Russian rubles, only dollars, was located on the first floor of our hotel and had many things available. We were able to buy coffee, baked goods, chocolate, and wine. On the way to dinner, we purchased flowers. Latvians love flowers — we couldn't arrive without flowers for the hostess.

After my mother had recovered from the flight, she was happy to receive a few reporters for that promised interview. When the reporters arrived, she had something even more important than pastries and coffee to offer them. She had brought with her several copies of Latvia's Constitution from the 1920s.

The joy and excitement that this gift stirred in them was a surprise to me. I was impressed that Mama had the forethought to make copies of Latvia's Constitution and bring them, with the hope of giving them to patriotic Latvians. We were told that they couldn't find even one surviving copy of our old Constitution after the War and occupation. They must have all been burned along with many history books - all a part of the attempted Russification of the Latvian population. Mama obviously understood the "cleansing" the Latvian nation had endured at the end of WWII and throughout the 1950s. One gentleman, who arrived later, asked for an extra copy. He explained that he had been searching everywhere for copies of the old Constitution. He and his friends were preparing for the renewal of their independence and thought that they would have to write a totally new constitution.

Mama said, "This is my last copy, but no problem. There must be something like Kinkos in Riga, right? Or, drug stores have Xerox machines, don't they? We can go make more copies." He was amused and smiled. He shook his head and said, "Xerox machines are only available in government offices. It would be unwise to show this to government officials quite yet."

I realized then that even Mama did not understand the absolute control a Communist regime will exercise over the public. *"No wonder my friends in America cannot understand how oppressive Communism is,"* I thought. Xerox machines could be used to disseminate information. Communists want control of all information so they can keep the truth from the public. When people are kept in the dark, uninformed or misinformed, they are easier to control.

The next day we visited the church where I was baptized. It had not been used as a church, it was a concert hall because of the exquisite, large organ. Mama's heartfelt desire was to see our summer cottage. Through Mrs. Skulte's connections, permission was granted and a car and driver were provided. Mama had made Mrs. Skulte's acquaintance in California, where she had traveled from Latvia with a choir. She had connections in the government. She convinced the authorities that since our father had suffered and died in the hands of the dreadful Nazis, we were not Fascists, we had not escaped from the Communists, "the saviors of the working class," as they saw themselves. Everyone who was not a Communist was considered to be a Nazi. Of course, we had to have a Communist Government escort, but we were delighted that we received permission to visit our former home and our grandfather's farm, Auci.

First, we were driven to Jurmala. As we approached the coastline with the car windows down, I was greeted by the familiar scent of the Baltic Ocean breeze mingling with the fragrance of the tall pines that line the seashore. Memories rushed back as if it was yesterday that I had played beneath their branches. Mama had been carrying on a polite conversation with our escort, but as we turned left off the main street onto the narrow lane that would lead us to Jewel Street, the conversation trailed off. In the quiet, with only the gritty sound of tires driving across pebbles, I realize all three of us were lost in our private memories and emotions. Then, there it was; right in front of us was the beautiful, overgrown waterfront lot and our home of so long ago. Our cottage looked as sad as I felt, I saw Mama's eyes fill with tears. My emotion of sadness was mingled with great joy, joy that we were able to be here at long last.

The garden was overgrown with weeds and brush that reached above my shoulder. Still, I recalled every corner of that place. The sadness returned, like a mist from the past, as I stood beside Mama and Anna in the bedroom that she had shared with Papa. She was not yet forty when Papa died, but he had been the love of her life. She never wanted to marry again. "My love for him didn't end because he died," she said.

Mama had fulfilled Papa's request, "Save our children," and she had done so much more than just save us. After touring the house, we wanted to go down to the seashore. Our Soviet escort said we needed to go out the front gate and down the lane. I did not dispute him, but without saying a word, I proceeded, by instinct, to make my way through the shoulder high overgrowth and I emerged directly in front of our old gate. Even our large old-fashioned key was still there, hanging on a hook to the side. "You were so young; how can you remember?" I have been asked that question more than once. I remembered even though the overgrowth was so tall that the fence at the back of our yard could not be seen. Once there had been a path through the garden to that back gate, I had run down that path free and happy then, a secure child of two loving parents. Mama had saved Anna and me during the War, and now we had brought her back to the place that had always felt like home to her. Opening that old gate, stepping out, and climbing the sand dunes among the stately pines was so familiar. A rush of emotions, too deep to put into words, welled up in my chest as I recalled the carefree games Anna and I played under the shade of the pine trees, and the joy and love that once lived in this place with Papa and Mama at home in that house. The beach was empty, we saw a sign warning people not to swim in the Baltic Sea. Apparently there had been a chemical spill at the Navy base the Soviet Union occupied.

Next, we were driven to Auči, my grandparents beautiful farm. It had been incorporated with other farms into one huge collective farm. There was no private ownership, instead everything belonged to the "Government." The government was the "overlord" and bestowed the title of "director" as a reward to someone for being a good, loyal Communist. That individual may or may not have an education in the area that he governed. Had the Director of this large collective farm studied agriculture? I don't know.

The once lovely, large country manor was now home to eleven families, some of whom had been imported from other Soviet countries and did not speak Latvian. All the adults who lived in Auči were laborers at the collective farm. A cinderblock stove had been installed in every other room, and the house smelled as bad as it looked. The tall tower of the house had been used in the war by both Nazi and Russian forces since it provided a vast view in all directions. One could see for miles from the top floor, across the flat farmland that lies along the shore of a deep river. Bullets from the war were still lodged in the large old beams, evidence of the fierce battles fought on our land by the Russian and the Nazi armies.

The apple tree orchards had been cut down. Most likely, the 11 families who had been moved into Opa's home, needed the wood to survive the cold of winter and to cook. Pastures, where sheep, cattle, and horses had once grazed, now lay fallow. Large fields that could be producing wheat and rye now grew weeds. Not only was the apple orchard gone but so were the beehives, which had provided enough honey for the family and with enough to sell. In winters at Auči, when Latvia was a democracy, the farmworkers still had a job. They baked bricks and shipped them on the frozen river to Riga. They lived in their own cottages on the property. Under Communism, the land was not well utilized, and workers for the County Collective farm lived in very poor conditions, all 11 families crammed into our country manor which had suffered badly in the war and was in great need of repair.

When we returned to Riga, at the end of the day, our official escort left us and we were able to talk to the driver who had chauffeured us all day. We wanted to give him a thank you present, something he needed or wanted — something we could purchase at the dollar store which he was not allowed to enter. It took much coaxing, but we would not get out of his car until he relented. After sitting in the parked car and talking for awhile, he realized that we meant what we said and at last he told us that he had not been able to find shoes for his two-year-old child. Communism had trained him well to be subservient to people with authority — Government authority.

Part of each day we attended seminars, which were presented by doctors visiting from the US along with local doctors and dentists. We were invited to see the needs of the hospitals. Some of the young doctors from the US were so astounded when they got to see equipment in use in rural hospitals, that they had only seen in medical museums in the US.

We returned to America, sad for the state of the dear old land we loved. Even so, we were encouraged by the strong spirit of the Latvian people and their determination to regain their freedom once more. Together with their neighboring countries, Estonian and Lithuania, the Latvian people were preparing to show the Soviets and the World their united determination to have their independence restored.

On August the 23rd in 1989 about two million people from Lithuania, Estonia, and Latvia formed a human chain that united the three countries and showed the world their desire to once more be free, free from Communist control and the poverty and the suffering that result. **They stood in a many miles long human chain and sang ancient folk songs. The "singing revolution" helped to bring about the freedom for which they longed.**

Auči War Ravaged
Anna, Katrina, Anastajia 1989 Visit

Chapter Twenty-Two: *Redemption, Restoration, and Renewal*

"Freedom has its life in the hearts, the actions, the spirit of men (and women) and so it must be daily earned and refreshed - else like a flower cut from its lifegiving roots, it will wither and die."
Dwight D. Eisenhower

That first trip back to Latvia inspired me to employ all that I had learned about providing aid to an impoverished country. Our Church's work in Honduras and Malawi, as well as among the homeless of our own city, was valuable experience that I could now employ to help Latvia. After forty-five years of Communist occupation, Latvia, in 1989, looked like an impoverished country.

Back in Florida from that trip, with Dave's support and approval, I established "Baltic Outreach." People from All Saints Church joined me in praying for this work. God opened the "storehouses of heaven" and provided doctors in Winter Park who invited me to speak at hospital meetings about the needs in Latvian hospitals, the need for everything from hospital beds to medication, to x-ray machines. That resulted in many donations from all over Central Florida. At church groups, I spoke about the needs in orphanages, where children were cared for lovingly, but didn't have any educational toys. They weren't prepared to live an independent and productive life as adults in the future. The money we needed to pay for shipping containers always arrived just in time. Through a retired antique dealer, God provided the expertise we needed to load the containers properly and safely. He had brought containers full of antiques from Europe to sell in his store. He taught me and our volunteers to pack a container from the floor up to the ceiling in about a five or six-foot section, then tie that off and proceed to pack, from floor to ceiling the next section, and tie that down and so on. The manpower to lift heavy equipment was provided by men in our church, who took the day off from work, along with university students — strong fraternity boys who took on the job of loading beds, mattresses, and other heavy objects in the container as a service project.

I flew to Latvia to meet most of the shipping containers and oversaw the distribution. Even so, on one occasion a vital piece of complicated dental equipment was sadly lost.

I worked hard, inspired by the conversation I had with an elderly gentleman in Riga. As a young man he had been in the concentration camp with my father. I considered it a privilege and an honor to sit down beside him and pummel him with questions. I could tell that talking to me about the "hell" he lived through cost him emotionally. He was quite elderly, but he understood the thirst I had to know about my father's last months on earth. He said, "Your father was so strong. He kept us from despair on days when our bodies were exhausted from hard labor, our fingers were frozen, and our stomachs ached from starvation — he would start singing folksongs. That revived us and kept our spirits up. I recall, on more than one occasion when a man had rolled onto the straw covered boards of the sheared bunkbeds ready to die, Professor Čakste went to him and encouraged him to get up, lift his voice, and move his aching limbs. We lived on one more day, one day at a time. We had to survive to rebuild Latvia, your father told us. It broke my heart, when on that death march, he succumbed to meningitis or typhoid, I don't know which, or both. He told me, as he was dying, 'You are younger. You *must*, survive to help rebuild Latvia.'" I cherished every word and I'm thankful to have met a couple of people who were with Papa when he died. A Catholic priest had given him Last Rites, even though my father was a Lutheran. In a time of war denominations did not separate Christians. In Christ they were united.

My father believed unequivocally that the day would come when Latvia would be free once more. He believed in the strength of character of the Latvian people. My father, Konstantin Čakste, was only forty-four years old when he died on February 22, 1945. His vision for a renewed, free, democratic Latvia was finally coming to fruition, and I felt an urgency to help in the rebuilding process.

When, at last, it happened in 1991, Latvia celebrated the end of the Second World War and their restored freedom. What a celebration it was! The atmosphere in Riga, the capital of Latvia, was electric. Young people, arm in arm, walked down the streets singing their national folk songs, with joy that could not be contained. The fireworks show expressed their explosive feelings. It felt like ten years of New Year's Eve celebrations wrapped into one.

After the celebrations, the hard work of a restoration began. Farms were left without tractors, and in some cases no farm equipment whatsoever was left as the occupiers moved out. Private ownership needed to be restored. The elderly, who had been required to send the first fruits of their produce to Moscow during their years of working, now were the responsibility of this fledgling, newly restored democracy. There were so many orphanages, for the size of the population, that needed to be cared for as well.

It seemed to me, that the needs were so great that my effort was just a drop in the bucket. Dave encouraged me. "Many drops can fill a bucket," Dave said when he sensed my discouragement. So, I persevered, my church community helped, and God provided. I was proud of the Latvian people — they were hard working and determined. They didn't want handouts, but they needed a hand up after forty-five years of the failed experiment of Communism as a viable form of government. Marx Communist ideology, Marxism, sounds like a very compassionate idea. In the Acts of the Apostles, recorded in the Bible, we read that at one time Christians held everything in common. I wonder, *did Marx develop his ideology inspired by the Acts of the Apostles?* I know the germinating seed was his disdain of aristocrats in Germany and Prussia and oppression of the "lower class" or the working class by those in power. I wonder, *did Marx read the Bible, the New Testament as a youth?* Marx was an atheist, his father had insisted that he be baptized as a youth, not because he had faith in God but because he did not believe there was a God. His father reasoned that as a "baptized Christian" he would have more opportunities in life. Marx did not want to live his father's hypocrisy. He was a rebellious, militant activist as a student. Eventually he was kicked out of the University of Berlin. After being exiled from Berlin and Paris he went to England where he developed the theory that if there was only "one class" and everyone work for the good of all people, the world would be a better place. That's sounds like the Acts of the Apostles to me, doesn't it?

The problem is that he tried to replace God and the reverence for God and His authority, with "the government". All governments are composed of people, and all people are sinful and in need of a savior. Inevitably corruption and greed and inequality resulted in two new classes of people: the people working in the government become the upper class and the governed, the citizens, the working class, those whose income supports the employees of the government, become the lower class.

As I worked to organize Baltic Outreach, Anna worked with the Latvian Red Cross to help children from large families access the education they wanted. She also helped Mother present the required documents that proved we were the rightful owners of our summer cottage prior to the occupation of Latvia by the USSR. All three of us spoke about the emotional connection we had to the cottage on the shore of the Baltic Sea. I thought it strange how the same place that still reminded me of my greatest heartache was also the place that enveloped me in the warmest hug whenever I had the opportunity to spend time there.

On one of my trips to Latvia, we had unloaded a container of mostly hospital beds. I needed help with the boxes of clothes, shoes, and toys I had used to fill in open spaces around the stacked beds and other hospital equipment. The hospital administrator sent a lady down to help me. We worked diligently for awhile, until she straightened up and said with a huff, "You foreign Latvians; why are you working so hard to send us your discards?" For a minute I was stunned. *I'm considered a "foreign Latvian?"* I questioned. Then I said a quick prayer for guidance. I knew that everything in the boxes was clean and in good condition. Some boxes had many beautiful brand-new toys for the orphanages. I didn't take offense, because I realized that I had not endured life under Communism as she had. She was much younger than I, and had no memories of what it was like to live in a free Latvia, as I had. Anything she knew about Latvia's independence would have been what her parents had told her if they dared to tell her anything. I had heard many stories about life under Communism. The government, (that is people who belong to "the party" and have unlimited power over the population) make the most basic decisions about your life. For instance, you can't choose to rent or buy a home. When you grow up and get married and want to move out of your parent's home you have to apply for housing and the government will decide where you can live and how much space should be allotted to you. Your schooling and your job all have to be approved by the government. Everyone has a job unless they are almost comatose. Women could retire at age 55 because by then their bodies were totally worn out. Everyone was considered equal; the joke was that "some were more equal than others." The Communist party leaders, in fact, were the new Czars who lived well on the backs of the working population. Yes, by this time I understood my helper's skepticism. I didn't take offense. I wanted her to know people who love God from a heart full of love. I said, "Let's open one of these boxes, and see what you think." We did, and she seemed very pleased with the contents. I suggested that she choose something for herself or her family as a "thank you" for helping me.

That evening I was back in our summer cottage in Jurmala, the very cottage which SS Nazi soldiers had surrounded when I saw the Gestapo arrest my dad and take him away in 1944 — the cottage where I had spent the first summer of my life, before the War, when Latvia was free. Even after all these years this cottage felt like home. It enfolded me with fond familiarity that refreshed my soul after a long day of work. I sat with a cup of Chamomile tea warming my hands and ruminated about life. *I have been referred to as a foreigner most of my life. Now some see me as a foreigner right here where I was born,* I pondered. Then I heard the Holy Spirit whisper in my mind this verse, I had read long ago, *"Consequently you are no longer foreigners and strangers, but fellow citizens with God's people and also members of his household"* (Ephesians 2:19). The lady that came to help me unpack the container and organize the contents for distribution had asked "Why are we working so hard to send us your discards?" My first thought had been that these are not discards, and I wished I had told her that people who love Jesus were led to offer "a hand up" to the people of a country I love.

Papa could have continued to teach at the University and ignore the atrocities that the Soviets and the Nazis committed against the Latvian people. He could have put his head in the sand and merely have said "hello comrade" or "heil Hitler," and just kept his own little family safe. He could have stayed alive that way. Because he couldn't live just for the four of us, he inspired me to believe that the good in people will ultimately prevail. He and Mama, inspired Anna and me to live generously.

Soon after we had arrived in Sweden, Mama, recently widowed, worked on aid packages to Latvian refugees in Germany while we lived in a one room efficiency apartment. I learned that to live for small, selfish comforts and objectives is to miss the fullness of life Jesus wants to bless us with. I enjoyed working on the shipments of aid because it had been a joy to see how God opens doors. He provided the man, a new parishioner at All Saints, who taught me how to pack containers. US pharmaceutical companies willingly donated big boxes full of things like Neosporin, sutures, etc. Doctors donated heart catheters, hospital beds, everything needed to fill many containers that had been shipped to Latvia, and the hundreds of people to help me, God provided. I have been amazed, surprised and overjoyed to see the generosity of the family of God. I have had the joy of meeting many impressive, interesting people who wanted to help Latvia get back on her feet. Anna has experienced the joy of helping people in their educational endeavors through her work managing her charitable trust.

Yes, my true and eternal citizenship is in Heaven, but God has a purpose for each of our lives and it is in fulfilling that purpose that we discover the depth of joy Jesus talked about and we read about in the Bible. God's Word contains promises upon which we, as Christians, can depend. The Bible is a priceless gift through which God speaks to us, to encourage and comfort us, to guide and to protect us. Too few people read it with expectation that God can speak to them personally through the pages of that Holy Book. I am glad that I learned reverence for the Bible as a child. One time I knocked the Bible off a table while chasing Anna around my grandparents' home. Apap stopped me and said "that's a Holy Book, pick it up carefully and kiss it and place it back where it belongs".

Many years ago, when I was exiled in Sweden, I heard that pastor read from the Bible, "God is the Father of the fatherless," I knew then that I belonged to His household, and He has fathered me throughout these many years. The country my dad died for is free — the people are free to choose their destiny. What will it be? All souls yearn for freedom because God created us with a free will. We read in Genesis that He created the world and said, "It is good." He gave mankind authority to exercise dominion, good stewardship, over his creation. His desire is that we choose to receive His love, choose to worship Him and love Him, and choose to obey Him freely. The souls of all people yearn for that freedom, but freedom must be coupled with responsibility and accountability to the Almighty. We are free to seek Him, to live in His Will, or not. We can only be free if we recognize our Creator God as King of kings and Lord of lords. We can choose no other ruler if we want true freedom. *Will this new generation of Latvians choose freedom and accept responsibility?* I wondered?

St. Augustine wrote, "Our souls are restless until we find our rest in you" [Jesus]. *"Oh, precious Lord,"* I prayed for Latvia, *"may this Nation, these strong, independent people, when they become restless, seek after you and find you. May they live under Your authority in freedom and unity."* I prayed this for America as well, the country that gave me safety and a new life of opportunity.

I was happy and thankful to be back in the cottage my father and mother built with dreams of retiring there someday. My parents plans and dreams were upended by the brushfire of Marxist ideology burning across the western world — an atheistic ideology which leads to the people serving government as an all-powerful provider. It is the tap root of both Communism and Fascism. People who adhere to those ideologies desire for one world domination. It destroyed many lives, including my dear Father's, and caused so much suffering for millions of people. That dreadful, frightening time of war when I was scared to death, when fear of imminent death overwhelmed me and I called out for God to save me, and our merciful Savior, Christ Jesus, allowed me, a little child, a glimpse into His Heavenly Kingdom, that glimpse has been my guiding light. I had done nothing to earn such a great blessing. I was redeemed by grace and blessed to encounter the unfathomable love of God. Because of that encounter I have the knowledge that God is near and I have sought, imperfectly, to the best of my ability, to let our Lord guide me. He has led me into a fulfilling, joy-filled life, and I am so grateful. As Jesus promised us, the Holy Spirit has been my teacher, my counselor and my north star. St. Paul wrote to the Ephesians in Chapter 2 v.8 and 9 "For it is by grace you have been saved, through faith, - and this is not from yourselves, it is the gift of God — not by works, so that no one can boast."

Because I experienced the love of God in such a deep and profound way, I never had to struggle with the question, *Is there a God*? I know He is. I have relied on Jesus's words to his disciples, "It is good for you that I go away because when I go, your Heavenly

Father will send you the Holy Spirit, the Comforter, to guide you and lead you into all truth." "*If I were God, I would not have given people free will*, I thought. *Look at the mess people have made of his beautiful world, the wars, the greed, the disrespect of their Creator.*" Yet, He still loves His whole creation, every person, good and bad, you and me, just the way we are, and He longs for each of us to open our hearts more and more to Him.

I went to bed in my parents' old bedroom. With the window slightly open I listened to the song of the wind rustling the pine needles, and I slept in the peace of the Lord, with no worries of foreign invaders crashing our door.

The desire of my heart to bring my father's remains back to Latvia was always at the back of my mind. I sought and received help from the Latvian foreign ministry and the Polish government. A meeting with the Polish Red Cross at Stutthof Concentration Camp was arranged. My cousin's son, Uldis, offered to drive us to Poland on this, my first trip to Stutthof. We were warmly welcomed by the Administrator and the Red Cross representative in the administrative building of Stutthof. After the brief introductions and chitchat, I was shown old ledgers where I read my father's signature. Tenderly, I traced my finger over his signature, feeling a lump form in my throat and moisture spring to my eyes. His fingers had touched that paper many, many months after the last time I had been able to feel his touch in person.

From the administrative building we were escorted to his barracks. I noticed, that the thin walls had no insulation against the cold. The dark cabin had no heating system whatsoever. I looked at the triple bunk beds, wooden slats with some straw on top. That's where Papa, and several men, had slept side by side after a long day of manual labor? Their bodies were weak from lack of food.

The Polish Red Cross had gathered much information from the few prisoners who had survived. As I read their documents, a picture formed in my mind of the day in late January when, with Allied Troops closing in from the east nearing the camp and from the Southwest, an evacuation order was issued. With emotions of hope, fear, and anxiety the prisoners quickly packed satchels of their ration for their march. First, they hiked to the Kashubian Alps, not far from the town of Zukowo. A blizzard developed, the fierce wind scorched their faces and bent the trees as they trudged on with the SS soldiers and their guard dog pushing — threatening them. The snow was soon knee deep. The SS guards shot anyone who couldn't keep up with the pace of the march. "Through the snow the rifle shots sounded strangely tinny as they echoed through the thick forest," recalled Mr. Narutis. As the shots exploded more frequently the dogs became more agitated and aggressive. Each shot announced the end of one human life. For days the blizzard raged on. In February they had arrived at a work camp near the town of Gans.

With our new Polish Red Cross friends as our guides, we drove the approximate path of the "death march" from Stutthof to Gans. Riding in the comfort of my cousin's car, on a sunny summer day, it was hard to imagine what it would have been like to walk all of that distance through a February blizzard, in knee deep snow. We stopped at a nice restaurant and I thought about Papa dipping stale bread into a thin soup made with horsemeat to get some nourishment for his body, as I ate my delicious lunch.

Back on the road, we arrived at a Memorial the Polish people had erected by the side of a large fertile field. It had been the location of a work camp during the War. By the time the column of prisoners Papa was a part of had reached this location their numbers had dwindle from 850 prisoners to only 250. At this camp Papa and 34 other men had laid straw on the floor of a small clap board barrack and slept side by side like sardines. They shared what little rations they had left. The "Angel of Death" was hovering over the camp raining down starvation, typhoid, and meningitis. Of the 35 men in his cabin, my father had been the first to succumb.

Inscribed on that beautiful memorial are the names of just a few of the distinguished prisoners who had died as a result of the death march. Along with my Father's name is the name of a Lithuanian Catholic priest, Father Lipniunas. I learned that this holy man, had insisted on carrying with him his Prayer Book and everything needed to celebrate the Mass, even though in his weakened state it made his satchel heavy. The night, in that field, when my father was dying Fr. Lipniunas had prayed over him and given him his Last Rites. I thanked God for that news, I was deeply comforted to know that Papa went to Heaven as his fellow prisoners prayed over him. Papa was a Lutheran, but to men standing at the gate of

Heaven, denominations didn't matter. We are all children of God seeking — seeking — seeking.

In our seeking for God and desiring to live a life pleasing to him, we tend to become dogmatic, even legalistic at times. We let "particulars" divide us. But there, at death's door, they had learned that in the end only one thing matters. God! What matters is that God loves us and that we love God and that we accept the redeeming grace of Jesus the Christ and that we extend that love to one another. That's the great commandment Jesus taught us; to love God with our whole heart, mind and soul and to love our neighbor as ourselves.

Walking along the edge of the fields we climbed a little hill. I had read that his companions had dug a shallow grave in the frozen ground on a hill beside the field for his burial. They had placed a closed bottle beside him in the grave. It held a piece of paper with the signatures of all the men present. Then they had placed a cross on top, made of wood they had found. Into it they had carved his name. I marveled at the huge effort all that work required, from men emaciated and sick themselves. I was told that by the time the Red Cross searched this hillside there was no sign of the grave or the marker. Nevertheless, I searched the area, looking for anything that might differentiate any portion of the ground, hoping, wanting! Pine needles, pine cones, moss, grass; my eyes scanned the area for any depression in the ground; it all looked the same. Eventually we had to return to the car passing through the fertile field that silently hid all evidence of the suffering it had witnessed.

We drove on to a nearby village where the prisoners had been housed in the school. There the local people maintained a museum to remember and honor those brave men. In a garden behind the school a cemetery had been established to properly and respectfully bury the remains of all the men who had died in that field in one large grave. I was told that, immediately after the end of the war, people were concerned that wolves or wild dogs or other beasts would dig up some of those shallow graves. What an awful thought that was. I certainly hoped that had not happened to Papa's grave, but putting his remains in a mass grave was also disappointing.

"With DNA testing we could identify my father's remains," I said, standing beside the large grave. Before the words had left my lips, I already knew the problem. So many men in one grave; we would have to find the descendants of each one and obtain permission from each of them to disturb the grave. With that realization an emotional struggle raged within me, and then, as I prayed and cried, peace returned to me, reminding me that Papa is not here, he is with our Lord, and he is well. It was a difficult surrender after years of writing letters, and contacting people in the Polish and Latvian government. I had had the pleasure of making the acquaintance of some very compassionate, knowledgeable people during my quest. It was hard to let go as I felt I must.

About a year later my sister and I, accompanied by our friend Dzintra Geka and her colleagues, were able to make this pilgrimage of remembrance together. We are very thankful to Austrums Academic Fraternity for the beautiful plaque they have erected in that cemetery. It describes my Father's work and leadership of the Underground Government of Latvia during World War II. Austrums Fraternity had preceded me in attempting to locate Papa's remains with the hope of returning him to Latvia.

My time in Latvia wasn't all work. I attended concerts and enjoyed the opera in the lovely old Opera Hall, with its gilded décor, that Mother had described to me. I drank in the culture, I resonated with it. I thought, I could *stay here forever,* but after several weeks I realized that I missed my family too much. My dear ones across the sea missed me as well. Dave, my husband of 40 years, loves me so well that he set me free to be away from him to do this work I enjoy doing. Every thought of him sustained me with deep joy. *It's interesting,* I thought, *there is a serious side to "happiness," — it's this internal abiding joy I know, it flows from the sure, unwavering love of God and love of my husband.* With joyful anticipation, I boarded a Baltic Airline plane and returned to the arms of the man I love and the children who waited for me across the sea.

No more than ten years had passed when I was pleased to be able to report to my church in America the tremendous and swift renewal that was happening in Latvia. Latvia no longer resembled a Third World Country. I concluded my report, as I conclude my story, with this: Perfect freedom can only be found in total surrender to the Lord of Love, Jesus the Christ, who gave his life so that our sins would be covered, washed clean by his blood. He has prepared a place for us as our eternal home. So that, in perfect freedom, we can approach the throne of God Almighty the Creator of the Universe and enter the eternal home prepared for all who received Him. ***"I go and prepare a place for you. I will come again; that where I am there you may be also". John 14:3***

And I said to the man who stood at the gate of the year:
"Give me a light that I may tread safely into the unknown."
And he replied:
"Go out into the darkness and put your hand into the
Hand of God.
That shall be to you better than light
And safer than a known way"

"The Gate of the Year" a poem by Minnie Louise Haskins

Auči Farm House restored

Katrina and Anastasia 1998

Anna, Father David, and Katrina 1998

"We are grateful for our cousin Jānis Čakste who oversaw the restoration of our grandfather, President Čakste's, farmhouse."

Katrina and Father David at the Summer Cottage 1992

ENDORSEMENTS

Beginning with the wry observations of an inquisitive child, author Katrina Čakste Wilson, tells the harrowing story of her escape from the Nazi occupation of Latvia. Her observations are full of endearing details, warm scenes from family life; but she does not shy away from the horror of all she and her country endured. The contradictions are intentional and present both the beauty and the horror in stark relief. Though I was only given 16 pages of the unpublished manuscript, I devoured them quickly and hungered for more. Katrina Wilson is a gifted writer.
Bishop Gregory O. Brewer
Episcopal Diocese of Central Florida

My friendship with Dave and Katrina Wilson for almost twenty years has been one of the great blessings of my lifetime. Their individual journeys are amazing, and their love story together is one for the ages! I am thrilled that Katrina's epic story has now been published through the providential connection of Bishop Keith Ackerman to Latvia and the Latvian Church.

While we grieve for the millions who like Katrina's father died in World War 11, we marvel that miraculous stories of survival like Katrina's story are still being told to the world. My own father miraculously survived ten months of captivity as a downed airman in World War 11. As such, Katrina's story touches me deeply.
Langley Granbery
Nashville, Tennessee

Share this amazing story of triumph over tyranny driven by courage, trust, and an absolute faith in God. You will be touched as you walk with Katrina through unbelievable challenges including an escape from the Nazi regime and an almost fatal sailboat accident. A triumph of God's love.
Bette and Bob McElwee
Franklin, Tennessee

This memoir by Katrina Čakste Wilson is a work like no other. Not only does it speak in first person of the atrocities in pre-WWII Europe, but it is a subsequent account of a life and death struggle to escape, ending in a miraculous and redemptive American love story. From beginning to end her pilgrimage reveals God's guidance, intervention and protection.

Our endorsement goes beyond recommendation. This is a compelling read for anyone who yearns to understand the Divine role in mankind's struggle to find truth.

Becky and Buddy Smith
Edisto Island, South Carolina

Katrina Čakste Wilson loves God as much as anyone I know. Her amazing life journey is a revelation for those of us who never had to flee our homeland as a child in the midst of loss and terror and find our way in a different culture, learn to communicate in with a new language and without the support of a beloved and remarkable father.

You will be inspired by this story of faith and trust that enabled Katrina to lead a courageous life in a beautiful partnership with her husband, an esteemed and beloved Episcopal Priest. This story of Katrina's fierce love and defense of her faith, family, friends and her adaptation and love for her new country are interesting and inspiring.

Pamela A. Peters
Winter Park, Florida

Katrina Čakste Wilson's story of growing up in Latvia during the horror of WWII is riveting. I could not put it down. It's one woman's remarkable story of the redeeming love and power of God. It will capture the hearts of those who read it.

Charles and Elizabeth Kown
Brentwood, Tennessee

Latvia, the Nazis and the Communists

In 1971 when my wife, our young son and I first set foot on the soil of Nashotah House, the Seminary in Wisconsin, I must confess that the words, Latvia, Nazis, and, Communists were not the words I thought I would utter. We were immediately taken by one of the remarkable and unique gifts that Nashotah House offers - namely praying, learning, and living in Community. As is the case with any institution, the newest members of the community have to recognize that there are those in the community who have been together for a year or two, and have just recently said "goodbye" to those who had just graduated. The newest members of the community now must see where they might fit in as it relates to the establishment of friendships.

In our first year, by virtue of how large the enrollment was at Nashotah House, many of us Juniors (first year seminarians) lived off campus making it more difficult for our families to see each other regularly. Early into our Junior year, a very kind couple named David and Katrina Wilson invited us to supper at their "flat" in the married seminarian housing section of the campus. It was obvious that Dave and Katrina had already lived an exciting life before arriving at the Seminary. An Annapolis graduate had married a lovely woman who was born in Latvia. Being from Pittsburgh, Pennsylvania means that my wife and I were brought up in an area where the vast majority of people had some type of accent, so Katrina's very slight accent simply added to her charm. Even though Dave and I were the ones called by God to be priests, it was clear to my wife, Joann, and me that God had His hand on Katrina, and that her vocation was obviously different from the one that led her husband and my wife and me to Wisconsin. I recall being struck by how easily they prayed out loud with others, and while one would think that this should be obvious in a seminary community, we must remember that we go to seminary to discern, be informed, and to be formed. In Chapel at Morning Prayer, Mass, and Evensong, we prayed easily together, but that does not always mean that we easily prayed spontaneously. The Wilsons did!

Years later, after serving remarkably in Colorado, the Wilsons went to an extraordinary parish in Florida. Joann and I and (eventually) our three children moved from Wisconsin to Long Island to Pittsburgh to Fort Worth, and then to Illinois where I was the Bishop of Quincy, following a Bishop who as Dean of Nashotah House had been a mentor to all four of us. Upon being invited by Fr. Dave and Katrina to Florida to speak, Joann and I were reunited with people who had, even in the one year we were together at Nashotah House, made a lasting impression. Once again, the words, Latvia, the Nazis, and the Communists came into our conversation.

Katrina had been born in Latvia. Her grandfather was the first President of Latvia. Her beloved father was killed by the Nazi regime, and her beloved homeland was taken over by the Communists. The escape of Katrina with her mother and her sister from Latvia to Sweden to Ellis Island, to….is more God directed and Holy Spirit led than almost any other story my wife and I had ever heard. This is Katrina's story to tell. This is Katrina's witness to God's grace that you need to hear. This is a book - her memoirs - that once you have read, you will never forget.

The Parish Press, which ironically was founded in Wisconsin, but is now in Texas is humbled and honored to help bring Katrina's testimony to print. It is our hope that upon reading this book, your faith will increase and that you will want others to read her words which we know will touch your heart. A cautionary note: you will cry, you will laugh, you will pray, and you will not be able to put this book down once you begin to read it.

The Rt. Rev. Keith L. Ackerman
Eighth Bishop of Quincy, (Retired)

It is exciting to read the experience of the granddaughter of the first President of Latvia, Jānis Čakste. Written like a novel, it is so much more - intertwined with historical, personal and spiritual aspects. As a Swede, when applying for Latvian citizenship, I had to learn the history of Latvia, the proclamation of the state after the First World War, and the first president was certainly described. The founding of the country fascinated me, and through this book, in a unique way, everyone can gain an insight into the processes that no history book contains. Anyone interested in history will find this book a valuable addition to the facts.

As a Christian, I especially want to thank Katrina for sharing the importance of the Christian faith in her dramatic life, which is full of a wide spectrum of events, from the horrors of war to the experience of love from God and so many fellow human beings. In her story, she does not shy away from painful experiences, because she has also experienced healings and ability to move on with God's help. The fact that her testimonies have now been written down, is a treasure to be shared and I am convinced that it continues to be a blessing to many in the form of a book. When reading Katrina's writings, one doesn't feel like reading but rather listening to her story because it is so alive, floating and personal.

As a bishop in whose diocese is the parish where Jānis Čakste was baptized, the farm he built and the square in the center of the diocese that bears his name, I feel privileged to have been able to follow the creation of the last part of the book, which is also a unique story in itself. When meeting in Dallas with Bishop Keith (also with Swedish roots), hearing that I come from Latvia, he told me about a man with whom he had studied at the seminary (Nashotah House, where I am currently also participating in one course), who is married to the granddaughter of the first president of Latvia. He contacted them after many years and learned from Katrina that during the Covid time Lenten season she had realized that she had to write her life story. It turned out that Bishop Keith together with his wife Joann run a publishing house and I enthusiastically supported the idea of publishing the book and hope that there will be an opportunity to publish this book in Latvian as well. One of the presentations of the book with the presence of the author will be in Dallas, where there will also be a delegation of Latvian clergy, including a pastor who is associated with serving in the Riga Cathedral, where Katrina was baptized. This is another example of the many testimonies of God's presence and guidance in life events, which the book is so rich with. Thank you, Katrina, for sharing.

The Second Bishop of Liepaja Diocese
Evangelical Lutheran Church of Latvia,
+Hanss Martins Jensons

It is with great enthusiasm that I received word of Katrina Čatske Wilson's book "War, Love and Redemption" detailing her family's ordeal in in the separation of Latvia from Czarist Russia, but also in dealing with great geopolitical upheaval throughout the course of her life. Her grandfather was the first president of Latvia, and her father was a part of the Latvian underground during World War II, eventually executed by the Gestapo. The Lord has called Katrina to "write," and this she has done. Her witness is indeed a testimony "...that nothing can separate from the love of Christ."
The Rev'd Canon Ed Monk, SSC, DD
Board Chair – Nashotah House Seminary

As Dean of Ecumenical Affairs in the Anglican Church in North America, I have had the privilege of meeting with and working with various Ecumenical leaders throughout the world. One of the most remarkable dialogues has been with the Church in Latvia. Having now worked with the Archbishop of Latvia, who is based at the Cathedral in Riga, and the Bishop of Liepaja, I have learned more specifically the challenges of Christians during the Nazi occupation and the Communist occupation. Seeing a Church rise from years of oppression is a source of encouragement to all Christians, but I had not read personal accounts of what life was like under such oppression until I was able to read *"War, Love, and Redemption"* written by the granddaughter of the first President of Latvia. Katrina Čakste Wilson's remarkable memoirs, by God's grace, are now a book. I am honored to endorse and recommend this book, hoping that others will become more aware of the plight of persecuted Christians, and even more aware of God's redemptive love and grace.
The Most Rev. Dr. Ray R. Sutton, Dean of Ecumenical Affairs
Presiding Bishop of the Reformed Episcopal Church
Dean of the Province of Anglican Church in North America